The Military & Society

Series Editor: Cara Acred

Volume 289

Independence Educational Publishers

First published by Independence Educational Publishers

The Studio, High Green

Great Shelford

Cambridge CB22 5EG

England

© Independence 2015

Copyright

Photocopy licence

British Library Cataloguing in Publication Data

The military & society. -- (Issues ; 289)

1. Armed Forces. 2. Military policy.

I. Series II. Acred, Cara editor.

355-dc23

ISBN-13: 9781861687210

Printed in Great Britain

Zenith Print Group

Contents

Introduction

The Military & Society is Volume 289 in the **ISSUES** series. The aim of the series is to offer current, diverse information about important issues in our world, from a UK perspective.

ABOUT THE MILITARY & SOCIETY

More than one in four new Army recruits are under 18 – is this too young or does the 'military ethos' have a positive impact? This book looks at the role of the UK Armed Forces, perceptions about the military and issues regarding military matters (for instance, woman in combat or what it's like to be gay in the military). We also consider life after service and address issues concerning ex-servicemen and woman such as mental health, homelessness and the care (or lack of care) for veterans.

OUR SOURCES

Titles in the **ISSUES** series are designed to function as educational resource books, providing a balanced overview of a specific subject.

The information in our books is comprised of facts, articles and opinions from many different sources, including:

⇨ Newspaper reports and opinion pieces

⇨ Website factsheets

⇨ Magazine and journal articles

⇨ Statistics and surveys

⇨ Government reports

⇨ Literature from special interest groups

A NOTE ON CRITICAL EVALUATION

Because the information reprinted here is from a number of different sources, readers should bear in mind the origin of the text and whether the source is likely to have a particular bias when presenting information (or when conducting their research). It is hoped that, as you read about the many aspects of the issues explored in this book, you will critically evaluate the information presented.

It is important that you decide whether you are being presented with facts or opinions. Does the writer give a biased or unbiased report? If an opinion is being expressed, do you agree with the writer? Is there potential bias to the 'facts' or statistics behind an article?

ASSIGNMENTS

In the back of this book, you will find a selection of assignments designed to help you engage with the articles you have been reading and to explore your own opinions. Some tasks will take longer than others and there is a mixture of design, writing and research-based activities that you can complete alone or in a group.

FURTHER RESEARCH

At the end of each article we have listed its source and a website that you can visit if you would like to conduct your own research. Please remember to critically evaluate any sources that you consult and consider whether the information you are viewing is accurate and unbiased.

Useful weblinks

www.armedforceslearningresources.co.uk

www.beforeyousignup.info

www.bootcampmilitaryfitness.com

www.britishfuture.org

www.britishlegion.org.uk

www.centreforsocialjustice.org.uk

www.theconversation.com

www.exeter.ac.uk

www.theguardian.com

www.independent.co.uk

www.kcl.ac.uk/kcmhr

www.no-offence.org

www.recruiter.co.uk

www.skillforce.org

www.standard.co.uk

www.telegraph.co.uk

www.ukdefencejournal.org.uk

Armed Forces information

We understand that many people are unfamiliar with the day to day details of military life, such as the roles of the single Services. To enhance your understanding of the Armed Forces, we have highlighted some key points that may be of interest to you as you develop your Corporate Covenant.

The purpose of the Ministry of Defence and our Armed Forces is to defend the United Kingdom, and Overseas Territories, our people and interests; and act as a force for good by strengthening international peace and security.

The Naval Service

⇨ The Naval Service consists of the Royal Navy and the Royal Marines.

⇨ There are currently 30,200 serving members of the Naval Service and also 2,600 serving members of the Maritime Reserves (Royal Naval Reserve and Royal Marines Reserve).

⇨ The Naval Service has five components: Surface Ships; the Submarine Service; the Fleet Air Arm; the Royal Marines; and the Royal Fleet Auxiliary.

⇨ 45% of the Naval Service is actively deployed globally at any time. It protects the flow of international trade on which our nation depends (95% of UK economic activity relies on secure oceans). Roles include: preventing conflict, counter-piracy, counter-drugs, humanitarian missions, stabilising hot-spots and building international partnerships.

⇨ The Naval Service is the most separated of the three Armed Forces. Personnel can expect to be away from home for 660 days over a three-year period.

⇨ Communication can be challenging. For example, the families of submariners are only allowed to send one 60-word message, twice a week, to their serving family member when they are deployed. The Serviceperson is not able to make contact with them.

⇨ Only 5,000 families live in Service Family Accommodation (SFA). The majority of Naval Service families live in their own homes, in civilian communities, around the UK.

⇨ There are Naval families living in nearly every county in the UK – they are not just on the south coast of England or the west coast of Scotland! The Naval Families Federation supports all members of the Serviceperson's family.

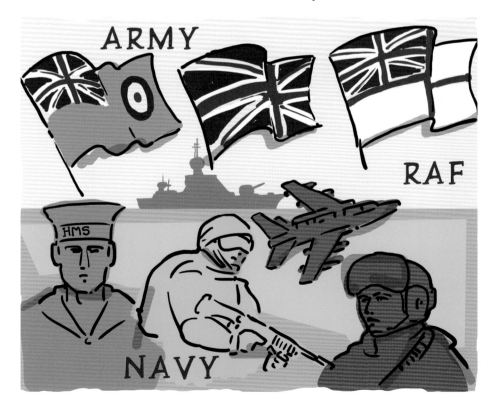

⇨ To hear some individual stories visit www.royalnavy.mod.uk/madeintheroyalnavy

The Army

⇨ The British Army consists of Regular Forces and Volunteer Reserves. There are currently over 89,000 Full-time Serving Personnel and over 24,000 Volunteer Reserves.

⇨ When Soldiers are deployed (for example to Iraq or Afghanistan) they are generally away from home for six to nine months.

⇨ Around 37,000 Serving personnel are married or in Civil Partnerships.

⇨ 10% of Army personnel live overseas with their families.

⇨ There are families living all over the world including Northern Ireland, Germany, Cyprus, Canada, Kenya, Brunei, France, Australia, Italy, the United States, Oman, South Africa and the Falkland Islands. The Army Families Federation represents them all.

⇨ On average an Officer will move every two years (often less) and other ranks every three years (again, often less).

⇨ 24,113 Army families live in SFA, with another 30% living in private accommodation.

⇨ Army families are based throughout the UK, with some living in remote locations, away from their immediate family. There may be poor transport links which can impact greatly on spouse employment and this can also cause issues with childcare or feelings of isolation.

The Royal Air Force

⇨ In 2015, the RAF will consist of around 33,000 full-time regular RAF personnel and 1,800 part-time reserve personnel.

⇨ The RAF's Mission is to: 'Produce a battle-winning, agile air force: fit for the challenges of today; ready for the tasks of tomorrow; capable of building for the future; working within Defence to achieve shared purpose.'

⇨ The roles of the RAF include delivering control of the air through offensive and defensive operations, and providing other supporting air operations, such as reconnaissance and surveillance, air transport and air-to-air refuelling. Our people lie at the heart of this capability.

⇨ RAF families are widely dispersed across the UK and around 65% of them own their own home. Others live in SFA on, or near to, RAF bases.

⇨ Nearly half of RAF spouses/civil partners are in full-time employment but, in 2014, more than half of them also reported that they found it difficult to find civilian employment after moving to a new duty station.

⇨ It's a complex, technical and varied business: our people are highly qualified, motivated and committed, and have a huge range of transferable skills. The RAF Families Federation is here to represent the concerns of all RAF personnel and their families.

For further information

Please visit our websites or contact us directly:

www.nff.org.uk | researcher@nff.org.uk

www.aff.org.uk | covenant@aff.org.uk

www.raf-ff.org.uk | enquiries@raf-ff.org.uk

⇨ The above information has been reprinted with kind permission from the Ministry of Defence. Please visit www.gov.uk for further information.

The role of the Armed Forces: delivering for Britain at home and abroad

The role of the Armed Forces is set out by the Government and it is the responsibility of the Ministry of Defence to deliver. This is done through seven overarching jobs that we call Military Tasks. Many of them overlap and are done at the same time but to understand our place in the nation's life it is important to know each separately.

Military tasks

1. The first of these is to provide strategic intelligence. Whether it is a ship or a submarine off an enemy coast listening to their communications, or an aircraft scanning the ground for activity and movement, or a soldier studying terrorist groups; providing that understanding of what is going on in the world is vital if our government is going to react appropriately. Alongside other parts of government we provide the nation's window on the world.

2. Our second task is the nuclear deterrent. We list that separately because it is our ultimate response and the final guarantee that Britain will never be an easy target. It takes huge effort to be ready every minute of every day but because we can never provide a guaranteed picture of the future, we must be constantly prepared to act.

3. The third is the most well-known task, what is sometimes called defence of the realm. It is the essential purpose of our Armed Forces to make sure the British people can live in peace.

4. This ties into our fourth task – because we are also here to help in times of national emergency. The police, ambulance and fire service cannot be prepared for everything on their own so, when needed, we help. That may include supporting the police if there is a terrorist situation, such as the Iranian Embassy siege in 1980, or helping ministries with national issues such as the foot and mouth outbreak in 2001 or the floods earlier this year.

5. Overseas our role is diverse too because we are not simply able to fight wars but also to build alliances. Our fifth role is to do just that.

To support British influence we carry out many different activities: from sending defence attachés around the world, to training foreign forces both abroad and in the UK. We also have many Service personnel demonstrating their skills with groups like the Red Arrows or our Military Bands. They too play their part in promoting the UK.

6. Perhaps the most sought after role from our friends – friends in the United Nations, the North Atlantic Treaty Organization, the European Union or groups of like-minded countries – is our sixth task: to provide expeditionary capability. Recently we have sent aircraft to the Baltic and a battle group to Poland to play their part in NATO exercises to reassure our eastern European friends that we will stand with them. In 2000 we sent a task force to Sierra Leone to drive back the rebel army and allow the Government to re-establish control. But this wasn't enough without our final task...

7. ...Providing security for stabilisation. Today's Armed Forces work very closely with many parts of government and none more so than, the Foreign and Commonwealth Office and the Department for International Development. Together we help countries rebuild after war or disaster. Sometimes we lend skills, such as our Royal Engineers; sometimes we lend strength to ensure those doing the hard work are protected. We did both in West Africa.

Together, these military tasks are why we have the Armed Forces. Everything we do is decided upon by Parliament and changes when required to meet the needs of the British people. For us, the most important thing is to be prepared to react to whatever is needed; wherever that may be.

⇨ The above information has been reprinted with kind permission from Armed Forces Learning Resources. Please visit www.armedforceslearningresources. co.uk for further information.

Why are our perceptions about the military so far off the mark?

An article from The Conversation.

By Bobby Duffy, Managing Director, Ipsos MORI Social Research Institute, Visiting Senior Research Fellow at King's College London

The image we have of our armed forces shifts between the three broad stereotypes of hero, villain or victim with different mental images dominating at different times and in different contexts.

Now, Ipsos MORI and King's College London are publishing a new survey on what the public in Britain, the US, France, Australia and Canada get right and wrong about the armed forces. The survey tested the public's perceptions against the facts on a range of issues: from defence spending, to the profile of recruits, the outcomes for soldiers returning to civilian life and the impacts of military service on health and behaviour.

Public (mis)perceptions

In Britain, we get a lot of things wrong about the military.

Two thirds of the British public think that Post Traumatic Stress Disorder (PTSD) is much more common among the armed forces than among the general public. Actually, studies show that levels are similar – yet only 6% guess this fact correctly. That said, levels are higher for those in combat, which may be what is driving perceptions.

The majority of people (53%) also think that the suicide rate is higher among the armed forces than the general public, when it is in fact lower – which only 8% of those surveyed correctly identified.

Over half of the respondents also think that former armed forces personnel are more likely, or just as likely, to be in prison when compared with the population as a whole when actually, they are less likely to be.

Hero, victim, villain

Despite this, we still have a positive view of the armed forces as an institution and of soldiers as individuals: 72% have a favourable view of soldiers and 65% have a favourable view of the armed forces.

This is not quite as positive as our views of firefighters, doctors and nurses in Britain, but more favourable than our opinion of the police and teachers – and, not surprisingly, significantly ahead of our views of journalists, bankers and politicians.

On an international level, attitudes towards the armed forces in the US are more positive (where 80% say they are favourable). British views are similar to Canada and Australia, but significantly more positive than in France (where only 52% say they have a favourable view of soldiers).

Overall then, we have variable and nuanced perceptions of the armed forces, with elements of hero, victim and villain dominating in different questions. The hero narrative around soldiers is still strong, as seen in their high overall rating. Indeed, in other surveys, the public see the armed forces as one of the top sources of national pride, just behind the NHS and ahead of the Royal Family. But at the same time, we think ex-service personnel are much more likely to be victims (for example, in terms of their mental health) or villains (in terms of their offensive behaviour) than the facts justify.

We often find this variety of perceptions and misperceptions when we are measuring views of a broad group, as our previous work on attitudes towards immigrants shows. In this survey, depending on the focus of the question, the majority of people see immigrants as both creating jobs and taking them from others. People can have many mental images of a single group or topic, and different elements are emphasised depending on where our attention is drawn by the question.

Suckers for stories

It's worth asking where these misperceptions come from – and whether they matter.

Some of it is simply our problem with maths. People struggle with relatively straightforward estimations, but much wider effects come from the biases and heuristics that we are all subject to when answering these types of questions – we grab for information, even if it doesn't quite fit. Social psychologists would say that our innumeracy can also be emotional: we overestimate what worries us as much as we worry about an issue we have overestimated.

All of this points to the significance of the media, entertainment and others who present images of the armed forces, such as charities and campaign groups. Studies show that there has been a stronger link between the armed forces and the 'victim' narrative in recent years, and that seems to be feeding through into public perceptions.

One of the reasons this content is effective is because people don't really base their concerns on a proper understanding of scale. We tend to remember vivid stories and particular cases, even if the incidence is relatively rare. Of course, these stories can be helpful in highlighting the real needs of ex-armed forces personnel. For example, shows like Channel 4's *Dispatches: Battle Scarred* have been vital in getting a focus on support, which is badly needed.

But it's a difficult balance to get right. Too much emphasis could have implications for future recruitment, the life chances for armed forces as they return to the civilian world and the extent to which the public support or even 'revere' the armed forces. Once mental images are formed, they can be hard to move. Misperceptions stick.

16 June 2015

We ask why young people see military as top source of pride

2012 was a year where British pride was at an all-time high. The London Olympics, Team GB and the announcement of the royal baby gave us all a renewed sense of pride, but behind these celebrations, the armed forces were always visible. Sarah Cottam of Loughborough University talked to a group of young people to find out how they felt about the armed forces after 2012.

Sarah Cottam is a student at Loughborough University, and a regular blogger for British Future.

The forces can, for many, be seen as the country's backbone, supporting everyone regardless of their gender, race, or in particular, age. There are constant reminders published in the news that someone's parent, friend, child or partner is selflessly risking their life, particularly for the futures of Britain's young people. It is therefore unsurprising that many people of our age have pride in the British armed forces, as they fight for our country, allowing us to enjoy such moments as the London Olympics.

'They are people who we can look up to, who are protecting our country and giving us a safe future,' said 21-year-old Tom from Loughborough University.

19-year-old Julia agreed, saying: 'the British armed forces have, and will, always instil a sense of pride and patriotism in me: the fact that a collection of strangers, all with different backgrounds, can come together and work with such efficiency and willingness simply due to a shared goal to support their nation, is something to be proud of.'

'To be a member of the British armed forces is recognised globally and I think that many people look up to them with the respect and appreciation that they deserve –

these sentiments are why most people will feel proud to be British,' she added.

Mary, from Durham University, said that 'having close friends training to be in the army, I am amazed at the level of dedication, discipline and courage that they show, as well as a definite sense of loyalty to their country. I think it is this commitment shown by all of its members that makes the British army so strong although it is not particularly large. It is because of these values that I am proud of the British army.'

20-year-old Ellie from Lancaster University also felt the same way about the armed forces. 'I think the armed forces make people proud to be British as it is inspiring to think that there are people who are willing to risk their lives for the safety of their country,' she said.

Matt, a student at Nottingham University, thought that the armed forces offered a great example for young people in Britain to follow. 'They illustrate a strong work ethic, a discipline and determination that many Britons have and they are incredibly proud of that.'

But beyond their work ethic, young people should also take example from their relationships with one

another and how they conduct themselves, he thought.

'They demonstrate the comradeship felt among the people of our country and a natural, almost modest willingness to preserve our way of life. They are unobtrusive and humble in the sense that they endure, they carry out their tasks with great efficiency and pride, an admirable quality that many young Britons have and try to abide by in their daily lives. Yet they are also amicable with a great sense of humour, and in that sense they are very down to earth. These qualities, among many others, make them the role models for our nation in the eyes of many young people today.'

The strong opinion of the group was summed up by 20-year-old Sam, from Loughborough University, who said, for him, the reputation of the Armed Forces 'creates the idea of the everyday hero'.

14 January 2013

Before you sign up

How dangerous is being a soldier?

This is the most commonly asked question at BeforeYouSignUp.info

A word about risk

The risk of being a soldier can't be known exactly because:

⇨ soldiers are posted to different places in the world where the risks are different

⇨ not all army jobs carry the same level of risk

⇨ it is impossible to predict risk in the future – for example, the Falklands War in 1982 took everyone by surprise and large numbers of soldiers were sent unexpectedly to fight in a short war that killed 255 people on the British side.

Every job in the army carries some level of risk. The most dangerous job in the army in Afghanistan was infantry rifleman, because the infantry were on the front line. A few other jobs were very dangerous in Afghanistan – for example, searching for and dismantling explosive devices. It is possible to join jobs in the army that carry less risk, but no job is without some risk.

Most common combat risks in Iraq and Afghanistan

Researchers asked armed forces personnel who had been deployed to Iraq and/or Afghanistan which threats they most commonly faced. This is what they found:

⇨ About half had seen someone wounded and killed (about a third had experienced this more than once)

⇨ About 15% had seen a comrade shot or hit who had been near them at the time

⇨ About a quarter had experienced an IED (roadside bomb)

⇨ About half had come under small arms fire

⇨ About three quarters had come under rocket/mortar/artillery attack.

For those in front-line roles like the infantry these experiences would be more common; in support roles like logistics, less common.

Risk of death

In 2009 there were 106,380 personnel in the army; 98 died as a result of their posting to Afghanistan. 71 of these deaths were from one part of the army – the infantry.

Over the course of the war in Afghanistan, the risk of death in the infantry was six times that in the rest of the army and seven times that in the rest of the armed forces. This is because the infantry were more likely to be involved in close combat and be nearer to enemy forces in general.

On the other hand, apart from the infantry, the mortality rate in the armed forces is similar to that in the population as a whole. This is because the armed forces are fitter than the general population and less likely to die from disease.

Risk of serious injury

The risk of being wounded in the battlefield in Afghanistan (for the British armed forces as a whole) has been about five times higher than the risk of death. This 5:1 ratio has been fairly constant, even as the fatality rate has fluctuated. For example, in 2009, 508 armed forces personnel were wounded in action in Afghanistan, of whom 158 were seriously or very seriously injured.

Again, the risk of injury in the infantry is much higher than in the rest of the army.

Of course, there is risk of serious injury in some civilian careers as well.

Risk of psychological harm

The risk of psychological harm in the army is higher than the risk of physical injury or death. A report in 2006 showed that about 4% of armed forces personnel showed symptoms of Post-Traumatic Stress Disorder). The rate was higher among troops with combat duties (6%) than those without (3%). There are several other psychological problems that are linked to exposure to warfare; these include depression, drug-dependence, alcoholism and relationship problems.

Summary

Most soldiers do not experience serious physical or mental harm as a result of their work but for those that do, life may never be the same again. These are risks that you need to consider before enlisting.

The pros and cons

There are pros and cons of joining the armed forces, here are some of the main ones.

The main 'pros'

Recruits say that some of the main benefits of life in the forces are:

⇨ New challenges

⇨ Global travel

⇨ Active lifestyle, including sports and adventurous training

⇨ Personal development and the chance to rise through the ranks

⇨ Physical fitness

⇨ Help with basic English and Maths skills

⇨ Secure job (for most)

⇨ Friendship and teamwork.

The main 'cons'

But there are down-sides of joining the armed forces as well. Recruits say that some of the problems of military life are:

⇨ Having much less choice in general than civilians, including little choice over when they can return to civilian life

⇨ Spending a long time away from home

⇨ The risks of mental harm or physical injury from warfare

⇨ Bullying and harassment for some

⇨ Sometimes disagreeing with the wars they are ordered to fight or with the way the wars are fought

⇨ Sometimes having to do long and boring jobs

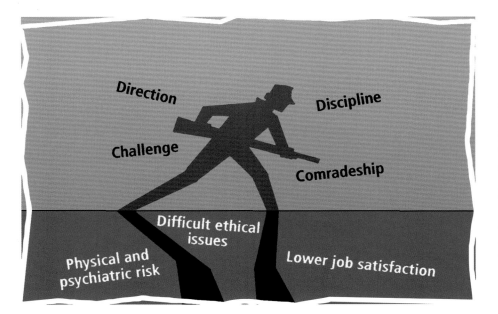

⇨ physical and psychiatric risk

⇨ lower-than-average levels of job satisfaction

⇨ difficult ethical issues.

Critics say that under-18s are less able than adults to make maturely responsible decisions, especially those involving risk or significant commitment – allowing under-18s to join the armed forces is out of step with the times. They might point out that under-18s are not allowed to join any of the civil emergency services, nor may they sign a contract (in England and Wales), buy alcohol or tobacco, or vote in a General Election. They also point out that the UK is the only European Union country to recruit 16-year-olds into the forces.

Either way...

Of course a military career can seem exciting and can work out well for some but it doesn't for others. Potential recruits and their parents/guardians should know as much as possible about military life before the decision whether to join, which should ideally be a fully informed choice made by the whole family.

The armed forces produce guides for parents of potential recruits; these can be helpful but do not answer the more difficult questions. Use the website and ask as many questions as possible.

Sources

D Gee, 'The Last Ambush: Aspects of mental health in the British armed forces', 2013; Defence Analytical Services Agency, 2010; Ministry of Defence, 2010; *Lancet*, 2007 and 2010

Armed Forces Continuous Attitude Survey, 2012; Armed Forces Pay Review Body, 2006; *Chartered Institute for Personnel and Development*, 2009

19 April 2015

⇨ The above information has been reprinted with kind permission from BeforeYouSignUp.info. Please visit www.beforeyousignup.info for further information.

⇨ Too many rules and regulations

⇨ Difficulty resettling into civilian life after leaving the forces.

How satisfied are people in the armed forces?

The recruitment booklets, websites and DVDs give the impression that everyone in the armed forces is happy but this is not true. There are more satisfied than dissatisfied people in the armed forces but they tend to be less satisfied than civilians.

Whether you loved or hated being in the armed forces could depend on:

⇨ The sort of person you are

⇨ What the people around you were like

⇨ The sort of job you did in the forces (there are many)

⇨ How well you were supported by your family and friends

⇨ What you wanted to get out of the forces

⇨ Whether or not you went in with your eyes open, which means understanding the pros and cons before you sign up!

Enlisting under-18s – the issues

Is it exploiting young people, who often come from severely disadvantaged backgrounds, to recruit them into the armed forces, or does it provide them with valuable opportunities to develop their potential?

A case for recruiting under-18s

Those who support military recruitment of young people under 18 might point out the potential of the armed forces to provide opportunities, perhaps especially to those who might be socially vulnerable and/or at risk of offending, addiction or anti-social behaviour. They say the armed forces provide:

⇨ discipline

⇨ comradeship

⇨ challenge

⇨ a sense of personal direction

⇨ a sense of public service.

The armed forces point out that where statutory services have failed to impact young people, the armed forces often succeed. They also say they would face severe shortages if they didn't recruit 16- and 17-year-olds because once young people reach 18 many fewer choose forces careers over civilian ones.

A case against recruiting under-18s

Those who say that the armed forces are bad for young people emphasise the risks, difficulties and restrictive legal obligations, as well as the ethical issues involved in training young people to kill. For example, young people joining the armed forces face:

⇨ complex legal restrictions on leaving

⇨ loss of some civil rights and freedoms

UK Military recruitment and selection overview

Introduction

In the First and Second World Wars, men had come forward to join the colours willingly or, later on, had been compelled by conscription. But after the end of National Service, and the demobilisation of the last conscripts in 1963, Britain's military needed to find new ways to fill its ranks, without an ideological enemy threatening it directly, or conscription.

With the discharge from the British Army of the last National Serviceman on 16 May 1963, the UK military became an entirely professional force. The end of National Service also meant that there was a need for the British Army to maintain its numbers of professional regulars.

As such, the UK military – since 1963 to present – has utilised a variety of methods to sell itself to potential recruits, which has also been varied across the service branches of land, sea and air. A regular fixture on British television was recruitment advertising including the slogans 'Be the Best' and 'Be Part of It' (National Archives, 2006).

Structure of the UK military

The UK military is made up of three Services (or Service branches):

⇨ The British Army;

⇨ The Naval Service (comprising the Royal Navy (RN) and Royal Marines (RM)); and

⇨ The Royal Air Force (RAF).

Each of the three Service branches is made up of both Commissioned Officers and Other Ranks, known as soldiers (Army), ratings (RN) or marines (RM) or airmen (RAF).

Due to a number of structural changes and economic pressures the UK military is increasingly utilising a Joint Force (or tri-Service) model of working. Typically the tri-Service concept is the removal of duplication and the standardisation of procedures, but also enables the Ministry of Defence (MOD) to make efficiency savings.

Manpower requirements

The MOD calculates the numbers that need to be enlisted to maintain each of the Services' manning levels. The MOD takes account of changing unit establishments, wastage caused by servicemen and women leaving the service at the end of their engagements, and those who might choose to leave before their engagements come to an end (PVR or Premature Voluntary Release). The number required in each trade in each Service is assessed and figures are published at six monthly intervals so that adjustments may be made during the year.

Traditionally, the Armed Forces have not met these recruiting targets. This shortfall in recruiting tends to be worse for the Army and for particular trades within the other two Services. For example, the Royal Navy has been experiencing problems in recruiting engineer officers.

With this in mind, the full-time trained strength of the UK military was 156,120 at 1 November 2013, against the requirement for a full-time trained strength of 160,390 personnel (DASA, 2013a).

By 2020 the UK military will have a full time requirement of 142,500 personnel (British Army 82,000, Royal Navy 29,000 and Royal Air Force 31,500) (DASA, 2013a).

The latest figures suggest that the UK military requires approximately 12,000 new personnel each year (DASA, 2013a).

Key points

Key points to note regarding UK military manpower include (DASA, 2013b):

At 1 April 2013:

⇨ There were 170,710 (trained and untrained) UK Regular Forces personnel, of which 29,060 were officers and 141,650 were other ranks.

⇨ The percentage of women in the UK Regular Forces was 9.7% in April 2013.

⇨ Black and Minority Ethnic (BME) personnel comprised 7.1% of the UK Regular Forces, continuing a long-term gradual increase in the proportion of BME personnel.

⇨ 56% of Army personnel were aged under 30, compared with 48% of the Naval Service and 40% of the RAF.

⇨ 1.3% of UK Regular Forces were under the age of 18, and 28% were under the age of 25.

In the 12 months to 31 March 2013:

⇨ 45% of all other ranks' intake occurred under the age of 20; compared with only 3.3% of all officer intake.

⇨ 69% of all officer intake comprised personnel aged between 20 and 24; compared with only 39% of other ranks intake.

⇨ The profile of outflow by age is to some extent determined by the nature of contracts under which personnel serve. In the 12 months to 31 March 2013, common exit ages for officers were 40 and over. Nearly 60% of all other ranks' outflow occurred between the ages of 20 and 34; however there is also a peak at age 40 which broadly corresponds with personnel completing a full 22-year career.

A general outline of the recruitment and selection process

Within the UK, individuals tend to be attracted to individual Service branches rather than the military per se. Each Service has their own identity, ethos, core values and standards and people tend to join the Army, Navy or Air Force. This is reflected in the way that each Service branch conducts separate recruitment and marketing campaigns. Each has its own strap-line (e.g. the Army's is 'Be the best' and the RAF is 'Rise above the rest').

Selection is conducted separately for each of the Services, but the selection processes are similar in nature. All three Services have different selection procedures for Officers and Other Ranks. However, all include interviews, aptitude and ability testing and some personality measures. There is a filtering system that will select people at the initial application stage, while others will be invited to attend an assessment centre which can last up to three days. As well as technical ability, individuals will be assessed on their general qualities to be a member of the UK military. In addition, preliminary medical examinations will also be carried out including checks on weight, eyesight and hearing, and individuals will need to pass a physical fitness assessment.

General eligibility

There are a number of eligibility criteria that must be considered before making an application to join the UK military and these vary across the Service branches due to the nature of the job/role an individual may wish to undertake. The general principles are outlined below:

⇨ **Age:** Every job/role in the UK military has a minimum and maximum age limit. The minimum age can differ between jobs/roles and is specified within each job description. However, the earliest application is at least 15 years and 9 months old when an individual applies, being at least 16 years old on entry and under 37 years old when beginning basic training (although the maximum age is typically around 30 years of age).

⇨ **Fitness Standards:** a 2.4km run (or two!) within a time limit appropriate to your age and gender.

⇨ **Medical:** there are various criteria including height, weight, eyesight, and checks for medical conditions and any ongoing illnesses.

⇨ **Nationality and residency:** individuals are required to be a national of Britain, Ireland or the Commonwealth. Documents required include passport, birth certificate and educational qualifications.

⇨ **Criminal convictions:** some kinds of offences and sentences can bar recruits from joining or rejoining.

⇨ **Tattoos and piercings:** these are dependent on location and nature and will usually need to be declared and shown during a medical examination.

When can an individual join?

If an individual is under 18 years of age, they will need consent from their parent or guardian before they can progress their application at the Careers Office.

If an individual is currently under a care order then the UK military will have to seek permission of the local authority in order for an individual to join.

Funding and scholarships

The UK military offers a number of funding and scholarship options which vary across the service branches, as highlighted below:

⇨ Sixth-form scholarship schemes

⇨ Welbeck Defence Sixth Form College

⇨ Defence Technical Undergraduate Scheme (DTUS)

⇨ Military Aviation Academy

⇨ In-service Degree for Non-engineer Officers

⇨ Bursaries (Standard and Technical)

⇨ Medical and Dental Cadetships

Get fit to join

Due to the nature of military training and operations it is critical that individuals get in the best possible shape in order to help them excel during pre-joining fitness tests, initial (basic) training and throughout their military career.

All three Service branches have put together training programmes designed to help individuals get their fitness levels to what they should be and increase their chance of success.

Tests and interviews

The UK military has a number of techniques designed to check the suitability of individuals for life in the military. These techniques are outlined below:

⇨ **Academic Ability:** although called different names by each service branch this timed test measures (dependent on service branch) general reasoning, verbal ability, numeracy, work rate, spatial reasoning, electrical and mechanical comprehension, and memory and is considered a fair way of assessing all candidates on a level playing field.

⇨ **Medical and eye test:** view General eligibility above.

⇨ **Pre-joining fitness test:** view General eligibility above.

⇨ **Interview boards:** a multi-day (2-day) assessment designed to assess whether an individual has the qualities needed to successfully become an Officer once they have completed

training (syllabus varies according to the needs of the service branch).

⇨ **'Other ranks' induction course:** a two- to four-day induction or familiarisation course for Other Ranks which enables individuals to sample 'life' in the particular Service branch (syllabus varies according to the needs of the service branch).

National Security Vetting

All military recruits will be 'security vetted' and there are three main types of National Security Vetting (NSV) checks and clearances.

Counter Terrorist Check (CTC): for individuals employed in posts with proximity to public figures, access to information or material assessed to be of value to terrorists or unescorted access to establishments assessed to be at risk from terrorist attack. A CTC does not allow an individual access to or knowledge of protectively marked assets.

Security Check (SC): for individuals employed in posts which have substantial access to secret assets or occasional controlled access to top secret assets.

Developed Vetting (DV): is needed for individuals with substantial unsupervised access to top secret assets.

Barriers to joining

A number of barriers to joining the military have been identified and include:

⇨ Misconceptions about the qualifications needed;

⇨ Lack of awareness of career options available;

⇨ Uncertainty about the type of training provided;

⇨ Concerns about military discipline and having to follow orders;

- ⇨ Being killed or injured; and/or
- ⇨ Disruption to family life and the belief that individuals are cut off from civilian life.

Criticisms of military recruitment

University

An article in the Huffington Post by George Iordanou (2013) suggests that military recruiters are taking advantage of students who are or may be struggling to pay their £9,000 per year university fees with the promise 'that their fees are going to be [paid] and a prosperous career in the Armed Forces is to be expected'.

However, the main thrust of Iordanou's vitriol is aimed at the universities themselves. Iordanou states: 'The presence of the military vans in Britain's universities is a form of exploitation… [and] …Universities [should] conduct their affairs by higher standards and should not be doing such concessions.'

Disadvantaged backgrounds

In an online article by Ekklesia (2010) based on an academic report it appears the British Army is targeting its recruitment activities at young people from the poorest backgrounds.

The report, produced by the London School of Hygiene and Tropical Medicine, part of the University of London, looked at army visits to schools in London and found that those with the most disadvantaged students are far more likely to have hosted military recruiters.

40% of Greater London secondary schools received army visits between September 2008 and April 2009. However, 51% of the most disadvantaged fifth were visited, compared to only 29% of the middle fifth. The article suggests that this news has sparked fresh concerns about young people from poor backgrounds joining the UK military due to severely limited employment opportunities.

Boy soldiers

The UK is the only European Union country to employ soldiers aged under 18, a practice opposed by the United Nations, and in 2009 the UK Government was criticised by Parliament's Joint Committee on Human Rights for continuing to allow the recruitment of 16- and 17-year-olds into the Armed Forces (Ekklesia, 2010; Forces Watch, 2011).

However, figures in 2012 demonstrated a significant drop in the number of 16-year-olds joining the UK military between 2001 and 2011 (Huffington Post, 2012).

Useful websites

Listed are some websites which the reader may find useful:

- ⇨ A very thorough document 'Informed Choice? Armed Forces Recruitment Practice in the United Kingdom' written by David Gee in 2007 and available from: www.informedchoice.org.uk/informedchoice/informedchoiceweb.pdf
- ⇨ www.beforeyousignup.info

- ⇨ www.gov.uk/organisations/ministry-of-defence
- ⇨ www.army.mod.uk
- ⇨ www.royalnavy.mod.uk
- ⇨ www.royalnavy.mod.uk/Careers/Royal-Marines
- ⇨ www.raf.mod.uk

References

DASA (Defence Analytical and Statistics Agency) (2013a) UK Armed Forces Monthly Personnel Report: 1 November 2013. Available from World Wide Web: http://www.dasa.mod.uk/publications/personnel/military/monthly-personnel-report/2013-11-01/1-november-2013.pdf. [Accessed: 04 January, 2014].

DASA (Defence Analytical and Statistics Agency) (2013b) Annual Personnel Report 2013. Available from World Wide Web: http://www.dasa.mod.uk/index.php/publications/personnel/military/annual-personnel-report/2013. [Accessed: 04 January, 2014].

Ekklesia (2010) Concern over New Statistics on Army Recruitment in Schools. Available from World Wide Web: http://www.ekklesia.co.uk/node/11072. [Accessed: 04 January, 2014].

Forces Watch (2011) Forces Watch Briefing: The Recruitment of under 18s Into The UK Armed Forces. Available from World Wide Web: http://www.parliament.uk/documents/joint-committees/human-rights/Briefing_from_Forces_Watch_age_of_recruitment.pdf. [Accessed: 04 January, 2014].

Huffington Post (2012) Armed Forces Recruitment Of 16-Year Olds Has Dropped By Two-Thirds. Available from World Wide Web: http://www.huffingtonpost.co.uk/2012/09/10/armed-forces-recruitment-16-year-olds-dropped-by-two-thirds_n_1871797.html. [Accessed: 04 January, 2014].

Iordanou, G. (2013) Get the Armed Forces Away From Universities. Available from World Wide Web: http://www.huffingtonpost.co.uk/george-iordanou/armed-forces-universities_b_4161976.html. [Accessed: 04 January, 2014].

National Archives (2006) Army Recruitment. Available from World Wide Web: http://media.nationalarchives.gov.uk/index.php/army-recruitment/. [Accessed: 02 January, 2014].

26 October 2014

- ⇨ The above information has been reprinted with kind permission from the Boot Camp & Military Fitness Institute. Please visit www.bootcampmilitaryfitness.com for further information.

Cadet force

By Shaun Bailey, Army Cadet Force 1983 to today, youth worker, government adviser

I was a member of the Army Cadet Force for over 14 years and have recently made a welcome return after being invited to be an honorary Colonel in the ACF. I have accepted this honour, knowing the life-changing experience my membership of the Cadets provided me with as a boy and a young man.

The Army Cadet Force made me. It demanded more of me than I asked of myself. It required me to believe in myself, to value myself and to know that with determination I could succeed.

For me it was never about a career in the Armed Forces. It was about serving my community. But first I had to learn the self-respect that leads to respecting others.

Over the first years as a Cadet I learnt more about myself than I did at school; I did not start out as top of the class, but by being a Cadet I developed the focus and self-belief to outperform expectation by gaining a degree. This made me determined to share with others what I had learnt as a Cadet.

As a Sergeant-Instructor I got that chance. It was the first time I was in a position where I could see the influence I had on others. It taught me about responsibility and duty. Like many before me, and since, being a Cadet was more than just changing into a uniform, it was about changing the way I thought about myself and our society.

Since then I am very proud to still be a part of the Cadet movement because of the opportunities it offers to all. Young girls and boys coming from every background become equal and part of one unit. The uniform makes differences in wealth or background disappear and allows all to work together without prejudice or stereotypes. This, for me, was liberation, as it continues to be for all Cadets today. For the first time I was regarded for

who I was and what I did, not where I came from.

Today, the values the Cadets taught me – selfless commitment, courage, discipline, integrity, loyalty, respect for others, adherence to law – stay with me.

I hope one day my own children will learn the same strength that comes from an education in what it means to be a citizen of our society; in fact, what it means to be British. I am convinced that the Cadet movement creates young people who are ready for work, and ready for life.

Find out more by visiting the websites below:

Sea Cadet Corps
www.sea-cadets.org

Royal Marine Cadets
www.sea-cadets.org/royal-marines-cadets

Army Cadet Force
www.armycadets.com

Air Training Corps
www.raf.mod.uk/aircadets

A day in the life of the Sea Cadets
www.youtube.com/watch?v=QwXZcW4jjVU

An introduction to the Army Cadet Force
www.youtube.com/watch?v=jC__wbD83El&list=PL00E822841B8172D0

An introduction to the Air Training Corps
www.youtube.com/watch?v=Diq2GxvyGUY

Cadet expansion programme
www.combinedcadetforce.org.uk/schools-expansion-programme/

⇨ The above information has been reprinted with kind permission from Armed Forces Learning Resources. Please visit www.armedforceslearningresources.co.uk for further information.

SkillForce

Frequently asked questions.

What is SkillForce?

SkillForce is a charity that operates in schools and further education, and draws on the skills and experiences of predominantly ex-Forces personnel, to inspire young people to succeed.

Who do you work with?

We work with young people between the ages of nine and 19 in England, Scotland and Wales. Most of our work is with young people aged 14–16-years-old, but also increasingly with primary school children and post 16-year-olds. We work in partnership with schools to shape programmes to the needs of students and the school. In general, we do this to deliver three outcomes for the young person: a) we bring the hardest-to-reach back into the fold; b) we engage those who need a tailored (more activity-based) approach to education and help them prepare for next steps in work, training or education, and; c) we help prepare primary school children for the step up to secondary school.

Why SkillForce?

We are the trusted provider in the sector. We have 12 years' experience of working with young people across the country. We get results because we understand that some students need a tailored approach. The empathy and skills of our instructors engage young people and, working with the school, lift aspirations and levels of achievement.

How does SkillForce work?

Our instructors work in school-time on school premises, usually one or two days a week. We have a range of programmes and schemes of activity-based learning which engage the young people, develop their skills and prepare them for the next stage in their lives in work, training or school. We tailor the programme to the student and requirements of the school.

Programmes can run for a short, defined period of time to help boost certain skills or levels of achievement, or we have longer courses which run over one or two years. It depends on the outcomes which the school and student are looking for.

What are your charity's aims?

Our aim is to inspire young people to succeed, working in partnership with schools and drawing on the skills and experiences of predominantly ex-Services personnel. SkillForce engages young people (mostly the hard-to-reach, those facing exclusion, or those disaffected with school), develops their skills, and prepares them for next steps in education, work or training.

Who benefits from your charity's work?

The most important beneficiaries of the charity are young people in England, Scotland and Wales, mostly in secondary schools. We are also working with a growing number at primary level and post 16.

Often our students are from challenging backgrounds or receive free school meals. We benefit those who need a more tailored or activity-based approach to education.

There are two other key beneficiaries. The schools we work with benefit because we engage some of their most challenging students, having a positive impact on the rest of the school. Finally, more than 70% of our instructors have an ex-Forces background. Our charity provides career opportunities in education for Service leavers through our 'Military to Mentor' programme, training and recruitment (including wounded, injured and sick).

What does it actually do for the young person?

We work towards three outcomes for the young person: a) we bring the hardest-to-reach back into the fold; b) we engage those who need a tailored (more activity-based) approach to education and help them prepare for next steps beyond school, and; c) we prepare primary school children for the all-important step-up to secondary school.

Our programmes help develop mental and physical resilience and raise aspirations. At the end of that journey, the young people are more employable, have greater awareness of their own skills, and are ready to take the next step in their lives.

We use recognised qualifications and awards as tools to deliver these three outcomes (e.g. First Aid, BTEC, NCFE, OCR and NNAS qualifications). This can benefit the student and can support the aims of the school.

We also have our own SkillForce programmes, and use our approach to complement the school's existing curriculum (e.g. SQAs in Scotland). These are designed to deliver outcomes agreed with the school. We can tailor our own 'Community, Character, Contribution', 'Ethos' or 'Zero Exclusion' programmes to achieve those outcomes.

What kind of qualifications can you offer?

We see qualifications as tools to deliver the outcome for the young person (getting them back on track or choosing their next step into further education, training or work).

In England, we offer a range of qualifications as part of delivering the outcome for the young person. In certain regions, instructors may also be able to offer other specialist qualifications. Once we know the outcome you wish to achieve, we would be happy to find a programme to make it work.

In Scotland, we are able to offer activity-based learning which complements SQA programmes. Again, once we know the outcome you wish to achieve, we would be happy to find a programme to make it work.

How do you work with schools?

We work in schools through a combination of on- and off-site provision. Our instructors work in and outside school hours, usually one or two days a week. We tailor the programme to the student and requirements of the school. We work in a complementary way (not an alternative way) to further the aims of the Principal or Curriculum Lead. The starting point is agreeing the outcomes for the young people.

What about employment for ex-Services?

More than 70% of SkillForce have an ex-Forces background. We also have a wealth of instructors without a Services background who bring experience and expertise in working with young people. We are always looking for committed, talented and empathetic instructors who can be role models for young people. We warmly welcome interest from wounded, injured or sick servicemen and women. Please get in touch for more information.

What do you do for the Armed Forces?

We have many years' experience of helping ex-Service personnel find a new career or meaningful work or experience in the education sector. The skills and experiences of many ex-Forces personnel are deeply valued, and can make an inspirational difference to the lives of young people. Having served their country, many want to serve their community. We feel that our instructors often benefit from working with hard-to-reach young people. We also look for opportunities for career transition for wounded, injured or sick.

What is the Military to Mentors programme?

Our Military to Mentors programme is a valuable stepping stone for Service-leavers considering work in education or working with young people.

SkillForce mentors have life experience and skills gathered from operational military service. Working in schools as part of a local team, our mentors take a professional and caring approach to inspire young people of all backgrounds to succeed. Skillforce mentors work with young people who are at risk of exclusion from school because of poor behaviour or attendance. The mentors help find solutions to their problems and offer practical advice when needed.

The mentors receive recognised training with qualifications: Mentoring for Young Learners, CET, Health and Safety, First Aid and Safeguarding/Child Protection. The mentors pay nothing. All training and work experience placements are funded by either the public, private and/or charitable sectors.

Aren't you a boot camp?

No, certainly not a boot camp. We have 12 years' experience of working with young people in the classroom environment, partnered with activity-based learning beyond it. Our instructors build a rapport of mutual respect with the young people they work with. It's about trust, respect and confidence. We find that gets results – not shouting or forced marching.

Do you wear uniform?

Yes, but not camouflaged military clothing. Our instructors in schools have a recognisable, smart SkillForce uniform. We work closely with schools to uphold standards of professionalism (and a positive image for the school) that members of staff, parents and students would expect.

What about external trips?

Elements of a SkillForce programme take place outside the classroom. We see outdoor trips and activities as an important way to inspire the young person to succeed. Often we learn by doing and experiences. All trips are rooted in the educational outcomes of the course, and are prepared with the co-operation of the school and students.

How do you measure what you do?

We start with agreeing the outcome for the young person. Then, during the course, our instructors collect data in the classroom every day (e.g. attendance, behaviour and attainment) which is analysed by SkillForce staff and shared with the school on a regular basis to make sure we are on track. We use feedback forms, questionnaires and interviews to make sure we are on track to deliver outcomes for the young person. Our *Social Impact Report*, which we can share with you, has more information.

⇨ The above information has been reprinted with kind permission from SkillForce. Please visit www.skillforce.org for further information.

UK under fire for recruiting an 'army of children'

MoD finds itself in the company of countries such as North Korea over use of teenage soldiers.

By Jonathan Owen

More than one in ten new Army recruits are boy soldiers of just 16 years old, according to the latest figures released by the Ministry of Defence. And more than one in four of all new Army recruits are under 18 – too young to be sent into combat.

The figures, released last week, have sparked renewed criticism of the British Army's use of boy soldiers. Following an outcry over the deployment of 17-year-olds to the Gulf War in 1991, and to Kosovo in 1999, the Army amended its rules stopping soldiers under 18 from being sent on operations where there was a possibility of fighting. Despite this, at least 20 soldiers aged 17 are known to have served in Afghanistan and Iraq due to errors by the MoD.

Critics claim the figures mean Britain stands alongside some of the world's most repressive regimes by recruiting children into the armed forces – among under 20 countries, including North Korea and Iran, that allow 16-year-olds to join up. They accused the MoD of deliberately targeting teenagers not old enough to vote in a bid to boost recruitment.

There are more than 1,700 teenagers in the armed forces below voting age. The vast majority of 16- and 17-year-olds are in the Army, according to the 2014 annual personnel report. And the proportion of Army recruits aged just 16 has risen from ten per cent in 2012–13 to 13 per cent in 2013–14. Many of them would have begun the enlistment process when they were 15, according to campaigners.

'By recruiting at 16, the UK isolates itself from its main political and military allies and finds itself instead sharing a policy with the likes of North Korea and Iran. These are not states which the UK would normally want its military to be associated with,' said Richard Clarke, director of Child Soldiers International.

And Paola Uccellari, director of Children's Rights Alliance for England, said: 'Targeting children for recruitment into the armed forces puts them at risk of serious and irreparable harm. The Government should not rely on children to plug gaps in the armed forces.'

Despite mounting pressure internationally, with UN bodies such as Unicef, the Committee on the Rights of the Child, and the UN Secretary-General's Special Representative for Children and Armed Conflict all in favour of the recruitment age being raised to 18, the MoD continues to take on 16-year-olds.

'Research has shown that 16-year-old recruits are much more likely than adults to suffer bullying and harassment, to develop serious mental health problems, to be injured in training, and to be killed once they reach deployable age,' added Mr Clarke. 'The MoD might think that it's a quick fix to use children to fill the Army roles adults don't want to do, but it's unethical and operationally unsound,' he said.

Critics believe a mounting military recruitment crisis in the armed forces is one reason behind the increases. Plans to create tens of thousands of reservists to fill the gap left by mass redundancies of serving soldiers are understood to be well behind expectations. Reserves currently number 22,010, an increase of 30 compared with 12 months ago. At the current rate of recruitment, it will take more than four centuries to meet the target of a 35,000-strong reserve force by 2018.

An MoD spokesperson dismissed the concerns as 'nonsense'. 'A career in the armed forces provides young people with benefits and opportunities, equipping them with valuable and transferable skills for life, so it is encouraging that young people continue to recognise this and are coming forward to serve their country.' The MoD has 'procedures in place to ensure no one under 18 may join our armed forces without the formal written consent of their parent or guardian and no one under 18 can deploy on operations'.

Colonel Richard Kemp, former commander of British forces in Afghanistan, defended the practice of recruiting 16-year-olds. 'Some of the finest soldiers I commanded during my 30 years in the Army started their careers as juniors, enlisting at 16.' The approach 'unquestionably boosts the quality and fighting effectiveness of the armed forces'. He added: 'Calling this scheme unethical and operationally unsound not only betrays Child Soldiers International's ignorance of military matters but also insults the young men and women who serve their country with courage, pride and distinction.'

But Madeleine Moon MP, a member of the Commons Defence Select Committee, described the increase in recruitment of under-18s as 'alarming'. 'The failure to recruit adults should not be used as an excuse to flood the Army with vulnerable youngsters.'

25 May 2014

⇨ The above information has been reprinted with kind permission from *The Independent*. Please visit www.independent.co.uk for further information.

Playing with future of British armed forces

Social scientists are to examine whether action figure dolls help form children's opinions on war and have a role to play in shaping the future of our armed forces.

It is the first time research has examined the role of toys in the making of young citizens. The £492,508 project is funded by the Economic and Social Research Council.

The researchers, Dr Sean Carter, from Geography at the University of Exeter, Dr Tara Woodyer, of the University of Portsmouth and Professor Klaus Dodds, of Royal Holloway University of London, have expertise in human geography, children's play, childhood studies, geopolitics and the culture of war.

The team expect to report their findings in 2016, shortly after the expected withdrawal of British troops from Afghanistan, which itself will inform the research.

Dr Woodyer said: 'This research project is highly innovative and the war play debate has not been addressed in this way before.

'We are not examining whether war toys are good or bad, or the psychology of such play. We will be examining how such toys help shape British attitudes to our armed forces, how do we learn to buy in the Help for Heroes, for example, and what ideas are children incorporating from outside sources, such as television news footage and children's films addressing war and conflict.

'The war on terror is being played out everywhere and since 9/11, our security and surveillance has come under intense examination. Understanding war, conflict and security in modern life is an urgent task for social scientists.'

The research will focus on best-selling military action figure toy range, the Her Majesty's Armed Forces (HMAF) dolls, licensed by the Ministry of Defence.

HMAF dolls are modelled on current British armed forces and the current best-seller is a ten-inch-high infantry soldier in desert combats. The doll comes with an assault rifle, radio, flak jacket, body armour, helmet and goggles. Its makers say the reason it has sold so well is due to the 'free promotion' provided by coverage of British military operations in Afghanistan in television news bulletins.

Dr Woodyer said: 'Play has frequently been overlooked as irrelevant to how people come to understand the world, yet it is precisely this apparent banality, the taken for granted nature of play that allows its role to go unchallenged.

'Toys, and how children play with them, are not just a response to the world, they help shape our culture.

'The role of action figure dolls has been unduly neglected, especially given the enormous academic attention focused on their female equivalent, Barbie.'

The research will include tracing the history and development of the action figure toy in British homes; the toys' role in wider geopolitical climates and cultures; bringing a social sciences perspective to museum audience research; and to develop resources for the V&A's Museum of Childhood, which is a major partner in the research.

18 November 2013

⇨ The above information has been reprinted with kind permission from the University of Exeter. Please visit www.exeter.ac.uk for further information.

Why Britain's Armed Forces are shrinking by the day and does it really matter?

More people are now cutting hair and becoming jihadists than opting to fight for Queen and Country.

By Joe Shute and Mark Oliver

The combined strength of Britain's hairdressers is now more than that of Her Majesty's Armed Forces. There are currently 185,000 coiffeurs to 159,630 regular forces personnel, and more troops yet are due for the chop.

The Ministry of Defence is implementing £10.6 billion budget cuts which will lead to regular soldiers being slimmed down from 102,000 to 82,000 by 2020.

But that doesn't matter, the Government says, because they are going to fill the Army gap with a minimum of 11,000 extra reservists by 2018. That means recruiting an extra 2,750 reservists a year by showing them snazzy recruitment videos.

The only problem, is since 2012, the trained strength of the Army reserve has flatlined. The MoD now says recruitment processes have improved. But even so, between April 2013 to April 2014, the number of trained reservists increased by just 170 people.

That means, by a rough estimate, more British people have travelled out to join ISIS in Iraq and Syria than helped bulk up our own reservist force last year. That's an estimated 400 to 500 jihadists, by the way.

Signing up new regular soldiers to plug the gaps is also well behind schedule. Over the past year the Army has recruited 6,366 regular soldiers against a target of 9,715. That's a shortfall of 34 per cent.

The MoD is now even looking at relaxing rules on tattoos on people's faces, necks and hands to try to bolster numbers. Your country needs you.

No wonder the Army restructuring has now been included on a Government 'Watch' list of projects Whitehall should be worried about. The National Audit Office, which scrutinises public spending for Parliament, isn't very impressed either.

A report released this month claims a two-year delay in recruitment software is actually costing the MoD an estimated £1 million a month, when all this was meant to save money. The restructuring, the report warns, poses risks which could 'significantly affect the Army's ability to achieve its objectives and value for money'.

It also found that Capita, the private firm with whom the Army has signed a ten-year £1.2 billion contract in 2012, is currently 67 per cent below its annual target for recruiting reserves.

A shortage of boots on the ground may be one thing, but at least we still rule the waves, right?

Well, we've got plenty of admirals (38) and captains (260) the only problem is there are fewer and fewer warships to accommodate them.

Lord West, a former First Sea Lord, has described the total number of escort vessels a 'national disgrace', and the fact we don't have any aircraft carriers as 'madness'.

But now, at least, we're finally getting one.

The new 65,000 ton HMS *Queen Elizabeth* is being named by the Queen in July and will be fully operational by 2020 (so that will just be a decade we've spent without one, then). We're building another,

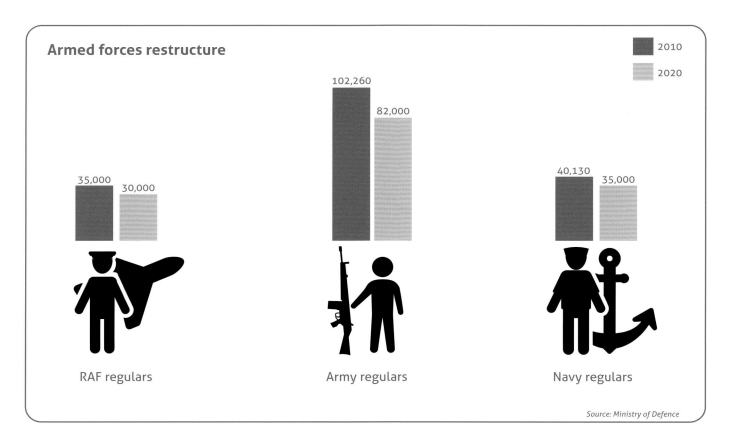

Armed forces restructure

2010 | **2020**

- RAF regulars: 35,000 / 30,000
- Army regulars: 102,260 / 82,000
- Navy regulars: 40,130 / 35,000

Source: Ministry of Defence

too. The HMS *Prince of Wales* will be ours for a cool £3 billion, except the Government is yet to decide whether to sail, sell or mothball her because it says it was committed to building the ship by the previous Labour administration.

Even if we do manage to keep them both, for the time being, at least, we're not exactly flushed for planes to fly from them.

On top of this, in 2010, it was decided to sell off Britain's entire fleet of 74 Harrier jump jets to the US for a knock-down fee. The plan was to replace them with 138 £70 million F-35 Joint Strike Fighters for both the RAF and the Royal Navy by 2018. But the plane has been dogged by cost overruns, delays and accusations of poor performance. Last week the Pentagon ordered all models grounded after engine trouble triggered 'an in-flight emergency'.

Mere 'teething problems', so claim military chiefs, who say the cuts will have no impact on the military force we once were. And, in any case, the world is a safer place these days; the call of duty comes increasingly less.

Yet people like these men... think it matters quite a lot.

They say Russia's actions in Ukraine have shattered the myth of European security in the post-Cold War era, and civil conflict in Syria and Iraq have left the defence reforms conceived of in 2010 outdated.

At a meeting of NATO foreign ministers in Brussels this week, US defence officials urged every member to now spend a minimum of two per cent of GDP on defence to combat the 'game-changer' in Ukraine.

At present, Britain remains one of only four countries in the 28-member alliance to do this (the other three are the US, Greece and Estonia).

But a new analysis commissioned by officials in the military and revealed earlier this month, has suggested this may fall to 1.9 per cent of GDP by 2017. The MoD insists defence spending will remain above two per cent this year and the next. But what about after that?

Only yesterday General Sir Peter Wall, the Chief of The General Staff, warned Britain may have to undertake military operations sooner than people think because of the rapidly changing security situation around the world. He also echoed fears that any further defence cuts after the 2015 election would endanger the Army's new slimmed-down structures.

Critics say these have been cuts made by bayonet, rather than careful scissor snip, and anything more puts national security at risk. When you no longer project power, the world stops listening.

But then again, maybe everybody will just leave us peacefully be. Nobody seems to give Costa Rica much bother. And they haven't had an army since 1948.

25 June 2014

⇨ The above information has been reprinted with kind permission from *The Telegraph*. Please visit www.telegraph.co.uk for further information.

British public demands greater spending on military

Boost for defence companies as new research signals British public want to see spending on military increased.

By Alan Tovey, Industry Editor

The vast majority of Britons believe that the UK should increase the amount spent on the armed forces, with more than three times as many people signalling that the defence budget should increase as those who want to see it cut, according to new research.

The UK currently spends £37.4 billion on defence. However, 53% of those surveyed by PricewaterhouseCoopers (PwC) indicated they would like that to rise. This compares with 16% who would like to see the budget cut, while 21% said they think it should remain the same.

The survey asked 2,000 people whether they would like to see the UK's military strength increase over the next 20 years.

The verdict delivers a boost to the defence industry. The UK is struggling to hit the NATO target of spending 2% of the country's GDP on the military.

The study – entitled Forces for Change – also found 37% of respondents believe the cost of funding the military helps to strengthen the economy, against 17% who thought it weakened it. The remainder were unsure or had no opinion.

The Army, Navy and Air Force are also perceived to be struggling to deal with the demands being placed upon them – ranging from traditional combat roles to humanitarian and aid work – with their current resources.

Analysis of key phrases and words relating to the UK military revealed a common theme, with 'underfunded', 'overstretched' and 'unequipped' all featuring heavily, the report found.

Roland Sonnenberg, a partner at PwC, said: 'The public take the view that the military's strength should be increased. This raises questions about how the actual readiness of the forces squares with how ready the public wants them to be.'

He added that although each arm of the forces is 'a multi-billion-pound enterprise in its own right', there is little data available to help the public to understand the military's impact on the economy and country.

Recruiting future personnel could also become more difficult. The report concluded that the lack of awareness about the military and the shrinking number of people in uniform meant fewer people have contact with anyone in the services to get an idea of what the job entails. Attracting enough high-calibre recruits could therefore prove a challenge.

However, according to defence think-tank the Royal United Services Institute (RUSI), the response was not surprising, with the first job of the state being to defend its citizens.

'Everyone will say we need an Army, but they do not necessarily have a clear understanding of what it is to be used for,' said Peter Quentin, who leads RUSI's land warfare studies.

Relations between the military and civil population have also changed recently, he said.

'It is not a bilateral relationship, of back and forth between the public and the forces, it's more like a triangle, with the Government making the third point – after all, they are HM's Armed Forces,' said Mr Quentin.

But recent issues such as a lack of helicopters and poor body armour for troops have 'distorted' this triangle, he said, with the public pressing for changes.

'Military personnel are being seen as victims of state policy rather than professionals, and the public are influencing government policy,' Mr Quentin said.

However, he warned against the notion that the public unreservedly supports a stronger military, with many people considering there to be a greater risk from how politicians may then employ it, citing the 2003 invasion of Iraq.

15 June 2015

⇨ The above information has been reprinted with kind permission from *The Telegraph*. Please visit www.telegraph.co.uk for further information.

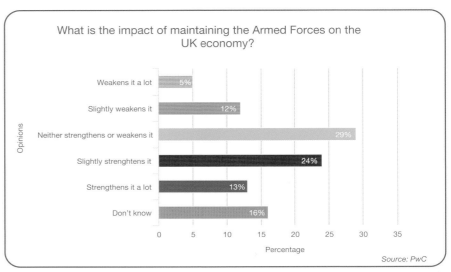

What is the impact of maintaining the Armed Forces on the UK economy?

- Weakens it a lot — 5%
- Slightly weakens it — 12%
- Neither strengthens or weakens it — 29%
- Slightly strenghtens it — 24%
- Strengthens it a lot — 13%
- Don't know — 16%

Opinions / Percentage

Source: PwC

Review of women in close combat roles: an analysis

By John Sayle

In May of 2014, Defence Secretary Philip Hammond brought the proposed review of the exclusion of women from close combat roles in HM Forces forward from its original date in 2018. It is now expected by the close of 2014. The current exclusion is, of course, divisive, with some commentators suggesting it is outrageous to have such a gender-discriminatory exclusion in the 21st century whilst others argue that the inclusion of women in infantry and armour roles would inevitably lead to an unacceptable lowering of standards, and that the military is not a social laboratory. Even military women are divided on the issue. Major Judith Webb (Ret.) stated 'We have to accept that we are different physiologically… We don't have the same upper-body strength,' and expressed concerns that allowing the odd exceptional woman who is capable of meeting service requirements to serve would open the way for less-capable women, reducing standards. By contrast, Brigadier Nicky Moffat (Ret.) describes the arguments against lifting the exclusion as the 'same that used to be trotted out to exclude women from the wider range of roles in which they are now allowed to serve'.

So what factors will the 2014 review take into consideration? The current terms of reference are:

⇨ An assessment of women's roles in recent operations.

⇨ An internal survey to determine current attitudes within the Armed Forces towards the effectiveness of mixed gender teams in ground close-combat environments.

⇨ The engagement of external stakeholders and wider society to determine attitudes towards women in close quarters fighting.

⇨ A review of recent research literature on the effectiveness of mixed-gender teams in a combat environment.

⇨ Consideration of the experience of other nations in training women for and employing them in ground close-combat roles.

⇨ A review of scientific literature on gender-related physiological issues relating to the performance of military tasks.

⇨ A confirmation of the legal position and a review of relevant legal cases since 2010.

⇨ An initial assessment of the practical issues and risks of implementing a change to the existing policy.

It is worth noting that these criteria will weigh not only practical issues but perceptual ones; the issue of whether the Armed Forces, Stakeholders and the wider public are prepared to accept females in close combat.

Some objections to women in combat roles centre around physical and psychological capability. Is there any truth to these objections? Scientifically, the answer would have to be a resounding yes. Some of these objections are patently ridiculous; hygiene is sometimes given as an example, which begs the question of how Neolithic homo-sapiens females survived without sanitary towels. Others argue that women are care-givers, not life-takers, and would be unable to kill the enemy in combat. Evidently those who perpetuate these arguments are unfamiliar with the story of Lyudmila Pavlichenko, a female Soviet sniper who amassed 309 kills including 36 German snipers during WWII, or Charlotte Madison, who was an AAC pilot and weapons operator on Apache Gunships. The first pilot in AAC history to call 'Winchester' on a combat sortie, meaning she had expended all of her ammunition, she said of herself: 'I've killed more people than Harold Shipman, Myra Hindley, Jack The Ripper and any other serial killer you can name all put together.' Evidently, women are not exclusively

care-givers. However, women typically possess less muscle mass, less upper body strength, and are more apt to break bones as a consequence. A 2012 study of women in the Israeli Defence Force established that female recruits sustained a higher rate of stress fractures than males, and identified causes. It was not the first of its kind; a US Army study found that the incidence of stress fractures in female recruits was four times higher than in males.

But the most serious objection is on the level of unit cohesion. There are a variety of issues associated with it. If a male soldier sees a female soldier wounded or killed, will he cease to 'put the mission before the man (or woman)' and go to her aid, or fly into a rage? Will men trust that women can carry their weight as an infanteer, pull the trigger when necessary and be able to assist them if they are wounded? When the inevitable sexual tensions and relations arise, what will they do to unit cohesion? Will a mixed-gender combat unit be able to fight effectively, and keep fighting effectively when they start taking casualties?

A review of scientific literature can allay some of these fears. The higher incidence of stress fractures can be combated by building muscle mass to support the bone; studies have demonstrated that stress fractures occur less frequently in women who are already active and train with weights – which would also promote greater physical strength to be deployed to infantry tasks such as carrying crew-served weapons or wounded comrades. For that matter, higher levels of physical effort can stop a woman's menses, putting the hygiene 'argument' to bed. Common sense can lay other arguments to rest. Sexual relations and tensions? We already have those in the British military. Women are embedded in combat units right now, add to which we no longer have a prohibition on homosexuality in the military. Given the low uptake of numbers in militaries in which women can serve in close combat roles, it is unlikely that removing our restriction will add any substantial degree of sexual tension or relationships to the battlefield.

One of the areas that the review will assess is the experience of foreign units. Possibly the most successful example of the integration of females into combat arms is the Canadian Armed Forces. Women are eligible for all roles, serve in armour and the infantry (the Department of National Defence is reticent on the matter of women in Special Operations Forces), and there have thus far been no issues with their capability, no lowering of standards and no negative effect on cohesion. This is not a new phenomenon – the order to integrate women into all aspects of the military barring submarines was issued in 1989, and Canada acquired its first female submariner in 2003.

How have the Canadian Forces accomplished this? Firstly, by not lowering standards; women in armour and infantry are required to pass precisely the same tests as the men, including running around fields with a fellow recruit in a fireman's carry. Captain Ashley Colette, who was awarded the Medal of Military Valour for leading a combat platoon in Afghanistan, hauled 15-stone men around in battle exercises. Secondly, after discovering that segregating men from women in training led to poor cohesion, recruits were thrown in together, without exception. Male and female recruits eat together, sleep together and train together – and they are taught by both male and female instructors such as Sergeant Brenda Hawke, a 16-year combat veteran in the Canadian infantry, who has served in combat arms in Kosovo, Bosnia and Afghanistan. Studies have demonstrated that groups that accomplish things – such as training – together have higher cohesion, and the Canadian experience bears this out. As regards perceptual issues, the manner in which the Canadian public accepted the death of Cpt. Nicola Goddard not as the loss of a woman in combat, but the loss of a dedicated and valuable soldier was indicative

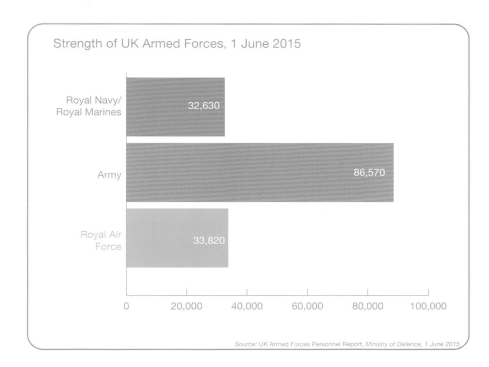

Strength of UK Armed Forces, 1 June 2015

Royal Navy/Royal Marines: 32,630
Army: 86,570
Royal Air Force: 33,820

Source: UK Armed Forces Personnel Report, Ministry of Defence, 1 June 2015

of public acceptance of women in combat; remarks made by Canadian servicemen off-record to a BBC reporter to the effect that they find the UK's attitude to women in combat patronising suggest that military acceptance has been thoroughly achieved.

An Israeli study, based on numerous sources of information available between 2002 and 2005, examined the integration of female combatants in the IDF. It reported that Commanders recognise that female combatants often exhibit superior skills in areas including discipline and motivation, maintaining alertness, shooting abilities, managing tasks in an organised manner, and displaying knowledge and professionalism in the use of weapons.

Denmark has had a similar experience – no difficulties arising as a result of integrating women in close-combat roles. Germany has had a similar experience – and since the Bundeswehr opened all roles to women, women appear to find a military career more appealing; even though few join combat arms; the number of women in the German Armed Forces has tripled since 2001 – a fact that will be of particular interest to the MOD given HM Forces' current difficulties with recruitment and retention. Put simply, we would benefit from a new pool of manpower.

But the British are not the Canadians, or the Dutch, or the Germans. Would gender integration work as well for us? In fact, British women have already served in close combat, as attached support personnel, and have done so for years; they simply haven't served in close combat roles. Substantial research into the British Army's experience of cohesion in teams that included females found the men in those teams noted no loss of cohesion as a result of integrating women. They even reported improved cohesion in non-combat duties under female leadership. Some of the women reported a perceived loss of cohesion – but these women were all recent embeds, new to the unit – they hadn't had a chance to achieve together, as the men had – and the study concluded that this was in fact responsible for the lack of perceived cohesion. One male infanteer characterised the continuing exclusion of women from combat roles as 'proof that dinosaurs still walk the Earth'. In fact, the study suggested that the only measurable loss of cohesion occurred when more than one female was added to a section-sized unit. At first glance, this would appear to pose a potential problem, but with the very small uptake of women in close-combat roles in other national militaries (Canada employs just 3.8%), it is entirely likely that more than one woman per section will never occur.

Objectively, it seems clear that there is no demonstrable reason why women should be excluded from combat roles other than some people don't want them there. Our own experience of integrated units and overseas experience of integrated combat-arms units indicates no measurable impact on unit cohesion. Physical requirements can be upheld to ensure that only women who are actually capable of performing the duties of the roles in question ever actually serve in them. The men who've served with women in combat have no problem with working with women in combat, provided they are up to the required standard – which can be accomplished by integrating selection and training fully, thereby also ensuring cohesion. Public and military perceptions are likely to be accommodating, or at least flexible.

Taken with the news that the US – up until recently, also proponents of excluding women from combat arms – have recently opened or are planning to open the Special Warfare Combatant-craft Crewman training for Riverine warfare roles, Basic Underwater Demolition/SEAL training, Ranger School and the USMC Infantry School (which has already graduated its first qualified infantry women) to female candidates, it would seem likely that when the review of women in combat roles is returned by years' end, it will recommend that the exclusion should be lifted.

Except for the fact that the majority of the information above, with the exception of the last paragraph, was available when the last review on this matter took place, just four years ago. The majority of it was actually in said review. And we're still excluding women from combat roles. So it would appear that the question is less 'should women be allowed to serve in combat roles', and more 'do dinosaurs still walk the Earth…'?

21 November 2014

⇨ The above information has been reprinted with kind permission from the *UK Defence Journal*. Please visit www.ukdefencejournal.org.uk for further information.

Transgender women could fight in combat as they have the 'physical strength' of men, says Army chief

Female transgender people 'might well be able' to serve on the front line, despite women being barred from combat, an Army chief has said.

By Louise Ridley

Women who have transitioned from male to female would make a 'very interesting test case' for the British Army, Lieutenant General Andrew Gregory said, although the force has never yet addressed the issue as it hasn't yet 'come up'.

Women are currently barred from serving in the infantry and in armoured units, but Gregory implied that female transgender soldiers could be an exception to the rule.

He told *PinkNews*: 'It would be a very interesting test case if it did come up. If somebody – birth gender male – who physically has all the physical strength and durability but had transitioned, they might well be able.'

He said there could be practical issues for female transgender soldiers in the infantry, explaining that accommodation may not be suitable, but added that the forces should not 'directly exclude' transgender people.

He said: 'We do not yet have any female transgender people serving in the infantry. We haven't had to address it because we haven't had the issue come up.'

In January, the Army's first transgender officer Hannah Winterbourne was praised for speaking openly about realising her 'body was wrong' while she was serving in Afghanistan.

She realised she was a woman while at Sandhurst at the age of 23 and has been praised for setting an example to trans people around the world.

Combat roles could be opened up to all females by next year after a Government-commissioned report recommended such a move.

Gregory admitted that there are still pockets of homophobia in the forces, but said he wishes to make the organisation as inclusive as possible.

The UK military has won several equality accolades in recent times, including last year being named the world's second most gay-friendly military in the world by a think-tank.

Meanwhile the Ministry of Defence won the most improved employer award in Stonewall's Workplace Equality Index.

It comes after Staff Sergeant Kate Lord, 32, was given a medal for challenging the 'highly misogynistic' views of Afghan soldiers.

She received the prestigious Queen's Commendation for Valuable Service for challenging the opinions of young men in the Afghan National Army, who accused her of being weak and said they were shocked that her husband would let her go to Afghanistan.

9 July 2015

⇨ The above information has been reprinted with kind permission from The Huffington Post UK. Please visit www.huffingtonpost.co.uk for further information.

What it's like to be gay in the Armed Forces

Just 15 years ago, openly gay people were banned from serving in the military – now the Ministry of Defence is asking recruits to declare their sexuality in a bid to improve diversity. One serviceman shares his experience of being 'out' in the Forces.

By Theo Merz

The Ministry of Defence is asking recruits to the Armed Forces to declare their sexuality, so that it can 'fully support' gay personnel, it was reported this week.

The information, which will not be released to anyone in the recruit's chain of command, will allow managers to see how LGBT people are being affected by new policies.

'The MoD proudly encourages diversity at all levels,' a spokesman said. 'Service personnel are now encouraged to declare their sexual orientation,' though recruits are also allowed a 'prefer not to say' option.

The move shows how much attitudes have changed in just 15 years. Before 2000, openly gay people were banned from service, and those who suspected personnel of being gay had a duty to report them to authorities.

Incidents of aggression against gay personnel are still reported. In 2013 it was reported that soldier James Wharton was threatened with beatings from servicemen in a rival regiment before Prince Harry stepped into defend him, while in 2009 the MoD was forced to pay £124,000 to a lesbian soldier for harassment she suffered in the Royal Artillery.

But the MoD insists it is committed to helping recruits achieve their 'full potential irrespective of sexual orientation', and all three branches of the Forces – Army, Royal Navy and Royal Air Force – featured in Stonewall's top 100 gay-friendly employers this year.

Commander Douggie Ward, 39, who is currently deployed on operations in the Royal Navy, shares his experience of being out in the Forces:

'People think we're still stuck in the Dark Ages when it comes to LGBT personnel. We're not – we're a reflection of the society we serve. Our biggest problem now is one of perception.

'I joined the Royal Navy as a logistics officer in 1997. At the time, I was living as a straight man and married a woman in 2003, so attitudes towards gay people weren't something I noticed as much.

'I did know people who were serving and gay, though, even before 2000, when the policy changed to allow them to be completely open. The policy before that didn't just affect them – it affected their friends, too, because officially anyone who knew had a duty to inform on them to the service police. The change allowed everyone to be more honest.

'I served in the submarine service, then qualified as a barrister and worked on the legal side in Afghanistan, Iraq and elsewhere in the Middle East. I also went back to sea as head of department for a destroyer. It's been a varied career, but also one that's quite standard in the Navy.

'In that time, I realised something was wrong and I wasn't happy. After a lot of soul-searching I realised I was a gay man. I couldn't live a lie and in 2010 I came out to my wife. She was – still is – incredibly supportive. We have two daughters, aged seven and nine, and we both still live in Fife, though I got married to a man in December last year.

'The next day, I sent an email to the other barristers in the Royal Navy – there are only 32 of us so it's a very small community. I told them I was a gay man now but I hoped it didn't change who I was. I was still a second-rate lawyer but now I was a gay second-rate lawyer.

'The way it is in the Navy, you go through a lot together so your colleagues are also your best friends. If I hadn't told them, people would have asked me why I'd left my wife, so I had the choice either to live another lie or tell them the whole truth.

'The response was nothing but supportive. There were some who I thought would have been indifferent at best, but the general feedback was: "Douggie, we thought you were going to tell us something important, like you were resigning. Of course it doesn't change how we see you."

'Every time I join a new team there's the question of coming out again, but LGBT people make that decision in all walks of life. Sometimes you simply don't need to.

'I was deployed to Afghanistan in 2012, primarily working in a US office, advising a US General. It was shortly after "don't ask, don't tell" was repealed so I wasn't sure how it would play. The guys in the office were asking me who my favourite actress was, and I said I didn't really have a favourite actress, but I did have favourite actors. It wasn't an issue at all.

'In the Gulf states, you have to be careful if a partner comes to visit. There can't be any outdoor displays of affection and you won't get a double room in a hotel, but that's just being mindful of their culture.

'When the Navy was looking for a new chair for its LGBT network three years ago, I volunteered, because the response to my coming out had been so wonderful and I wanted everyone to have the same reception I have.

'I never hear of negative receptions, really. We do live in a culture of banter so people will say things like "that's so gay", but I challenge it when I hear it. It's low-level stuff and not unique to the Navy in any way.

'From the older generations there can be homophobic attitudes. You only have to look on the Navy's own Facebook page for comments where an old-timer will say "that's disgusting", but these people are no longer serving.

'People have nothing to fear with the question asking them to declare their sexuality. Your commanding officer doesn't have access to that information – your best mate doesn't have access to that information. If you can be yourself 100 per cent, if you can be authentic, then you will be able to concentrate on the job in hand.

'People know when you're not being honest with them – when people come out it enhances the bond in that team because you're not hiding anything. What's important in the Royal Navy is that you're part of a team and you can do your job. Nothing else matters.'

17 January 2015

⇨ The above information has been reprinted with kind permission from *The Telegraph*. Please visit www.telegraph.co.uk for further information.

British Army to recruit more Muslims, ethnic minorities

The British Army has admitted its recruitment of ethnic minorities is not as good as it should be and is to put greater emphasis on doing so, particularly the recruitment of Muslims.

The Guardian and Sky News are among outlets reporting that just 0.54% of the army is Muslim, compared to 4.4% of the UK population.

According to *The Guardian*, resistance from Muslims to join the force is partly due to the UK's involvement in conflicts in Iraq and Afghanistan.

About 10% of the army is made up of black, Asian and ethnic minority people but many have joined from Commonwealth countries rather than the UK.

According to the media reports, the army has been trying to engage with communities with high Muslim populations.

General Sir Nicholas Carter, chief of the general staff, said in a statement provided to *Recruiter*: 'Our recruitment from the black, Asian and minority ethnic communities has been improving over the years, but it is nowhere near where it needs to be. We have to do more.'

The Ministry of Defence last year [July 2014] launched the Armed Forces Muslim Forum to help facilitate more dialogue with Muslim communities and encourage more people to join the forces.

Imam Asim Hafiz OBE MA, Islamic religious adviser to the chief of defence staff and service chiefs, said in another statement provided to *Recruiter*: 'Diversity is one of our nation's greatest strengths and it is only right that our armed forces benefit from that capital. This not only brings them closer to the people that they serve, but also enhances the military's cultural understanding when deployed.

'In my view, the values of the armed forces are fully compatible with the values of Islam as well as other faiths. Anybody wishing to pursue a career in the services, regular or reserve, and is prepared to work hard can be assured of a very rewarding experience.'

9 February 2015

⇨ The above information has been reprinted with kind permission from *Recruiter*. Please visit www.recruiter.co.uk for further information.

Doing our duty?

Improving transitions for military leavers.

Executive summary

This report examines how and why the lives of some service personnel fall apart on leaving the British Armed Forces, asks how they can be rebuilt and presents solutions to prevent these personal tragedies.

On average over the previous six years, an average of more than 20,000 personnel have left the UK Armed Forces each year. For some, transition is a difficult and complicated process. As a result:

⇨ Unemployment amongst ex-service personnel aged 18–49 is twice the national average;

⇨ A range of studies have suggested that former members of the Armed Forces account for between 3.5 and ten per cent of the prison population;

⇨ Estimates suggest that as many as six per cent of the current UK homeless population could be ex-Armed Forces;

⇨ Problematic alcohol consumption disproportionately impacts veterans and their families. This is a continuation of patterns of behaviour established whilst in uniform, where 67 per cent of men and 49 per cent of women in the British Armed Forces engage in hazardous drinking. These rates are far higher rates than those found in their civilian counterparts – 38 and 16 per cent for men and women, respectively;

⇨ Male soldiers under 30 are three times more likely to be convicted of violent offences, and those who have seen combat in Iraq and Afghanistan are more than twice as likely to commit a violent offence than those in non-frontline roles. These are sobering statistics after more than a decade of war;

⇨ Typically servicemen seeking help from combat stress have been through the break-up of at least one marriage.

Many of these issues are rooted in the disadvantage some recruits face before they enter service; research suggests that of the non-officer personnel in the military, 69 per cent were found to have come from a broken home; 50 per cent were classified as coming from a deprived background; and 16 per cent had been long-term unemployed before joining. More than a third of Early Service Leavers (ESLs) – those who leave having served less than four years – have endured the highest levels of childhood adversity. This disadvantage is often sheltered whilst in the military, but military careers are finite. In 2009/10, 60 per cent of those leaving the UK Armed Forces had served six years or less. The problems and consequences of such disadvantage can therefore

lie dormant until after the service leaver is discharged from the Armed Forces.

This report is based around five key issues that confront some service leavers, and it explores the barriers that exist to their successful re-integration at their point of discharge, and examines the consequences of failing to overcome them. They are:

⇒ Employment

⇒ Housing and homelessness

⇒ Alcohol and drug use

⇒ Mental health

⇒ Crime.

Negative outcomes in these areas are a terrible reality for some current and future service leavers. This report will tackle why and how this is the case, identify where they are most common in the Armed Forces, and make recommendations on how they can be avoided.

Chapter 1: Employment

The Career Transition Partnership (CTP), the current providers of transition services to the MoD, estimate that the overall annual employment rate amongst service leavers who have used the service since 2009/10 to be 85 per cent. The most recently available figures show that within six months of leaving the Armed Forces nine per cent of the 3,650 UK Regulars who used the CTP resettlement services in 2012/13 were unemployed.

Since 2011 the military has embarked upon a process of downsizing, including substantial redundancies, which will see the loss of 33,000 jobs. For those being made redundant, the situation appears to be getting worse. The unemployment rate rose to eight per cent for those in the second phase of redundancies in 2012, up from three per cent for those made unemployed in the first round in 2011.

Many service personnel lack the basic skills which are required for much post-military employment. 80 per cent of new recruits to the Army between July 2012 and June 2013 possessed the reading age of a 14-year-old or below. It is a problem that also affects the serving military; 39 per cent of serving members of the Army have the literacy of an 11-year-old. It is estimated that around 20,000 soldiers may have left the Army in the four years between September 2009 and September 2013 without basic functioning skills. A generation of service leavers is therefore at risk of struggling in their post-military lives.

Other barriers include the cultural divide that prevents accurate skill translation and an inability to equate or utilise qualifications gained in the military with those required by civilian employers. There are also problems of perception. 91 per cent of the public think that it is quite or very common that those who have served in the Armed Forces will have some kind of physical, emotional, or mental health problem as a result of their service – a damaging assumption for civilian employers to hold.

Chapter 2: Housing and homelessness

Currently, the main focus of transition services is post-military employment, with housing a distant second.

The Centre for Social Justice (CSJ) has learned that a particularly vulnerable group of military service leavers – those who have served for shorter periods of time and came from socially and economically disadvantaged backgrounds – are disproportionately disadvantaged when it comes to securing accommodation after their service careers. Their behaviour following discharge, of simply staying with friends or relatives, also has the potential to increase instability.

Many service leavers rely on the provision of the Armed Forces Covenant when they leave the military, which grants them special dispensation when applying for social housing. It states that: 'Members of the Armed Forces Community should have the same access to social housing and other housing schemes as any other citizen, and not be disadvantaged in that respect by the requirement for mobility whilst in service.' In theory, therefore, service leavers are able to circumnavigate the requirement to have a local connection when applying for social housing that would otherwise exclude them, giving them a greater freedom in their choice of where to live. However, extensive waiting lists, and a failure to ascertain an individual's service history prevent many from achieving this.

Housing for service leavers is a neglected aspect of transition. Insufficient attention is paid during the transition process to where a service leaver is going to live after discharge; it is too often assumed by the military hierarchy that they will find somewhere. In addition, the CSJ has learned from charities that there is a real lack of understanding about the housing process amongst service leavers. Too many service leavers, when faced with transition, assume that they will simply be given a council house by the local authority of the area they choose to move to on the day of their discharge. This assumption is both false and harmful. With five million people on social housing waiting lists in England alone, there is a major shortage that means, no matter how much veterans are prioritised, they will not get a property immediately after they leave.

Sadly, many service leavers can end up homeless as a consequence. Dr Hugh Milroy, CEO of the charity Veterans Aid, told the CSJ that in his experience around one in 30 homeless people in the UK served in the British Armed Forces.

Homelessness in former Armed Forces personnel is bound up in several complex and interlocking problems. Issues such as financial difficulties, alcohol abuse, mental ill-health and family breakdown all contribute to homelessness as well as being consequences of it. For example, the Ex-Service Action Group on Homelessness found that the homeless who had previously served in the Armed Forces were more likely to misuse alcohol than those who had not. The presence of such issues makes re-housing these individuals and turning their lives around when they present to charities such as Veteran's Aid in London or SPACES in Catterick a far more difficult task.

Chapter 3: Alcohol and drug use

Issues surrounding alcohol and drug abuse disproportionately impact veterans and their families. Within this, it is alcohol that creates the most significant problems.

Many members of the Armed Forces, serving and former, have a problematic relationship with alcohol:

'Although alcohol has always played a significant role in military life, the harm caused by heavy and sustained consumption is now well known. Excessive alcohol use may mask existing mental health problems, lead to dependence and is associated with violence and criminal activity.'

Research published in 2007 found levels of alcohol consumption that are hazardous to physical and mental health amongst 67 per cent of men and 49 per cent of women in the British Armed Forces, far higher rates than those found in their civilian counterparts of 38 and 16 per cent for men and women, respectively.

In contrast, in 2012, random drug tests suggested that less than one per cent of the Armed Forces used illegal drugs. This compares with 8.2 per cent of the adult population of England and Wales that have used illegal drugs other than alcohol in the past year.

A 2010 investigation of UK troops deployed to Afghanistan and/or Iraq found that military personnel were also more likely to report alcohol misuse after deployment than their colleagues who had not been deployed. Alcohol misuse was greatest amongst those who had been deployed in a combat role, and had been at greatest risk of being killed or injured. 22.5 per cent of regular personnel who had been deployed in such roles reported alcohol misuse, versus 10.9 per

cent of those who had not been deployed – more than double.

Service personnel under the age of 25 who had been deployed were also the dominant group in presenting with alcohol misuse issues, with a 2010 study finding that 26 per cent engaged in harmful drinking as compared to an average of 11 per cent across all older age groups. It is this group that the CSJ has identified as being more vulnerable to suffering challenges in transition.

Charities have reported the strong link between alcohol misuse and abuse and subsequent negative social, physical and psychological issues. A survey of those former members of the Armed Forces personnel in contact with Combat Stress found that 20 per cent were drinking at a hazardous level and 27 per cent were considered to be alcohol dependent. Similarly, Surf Action, a charity who works with veterans, told the CSJ that, as of October 2013, 100 per cent of their client base had issues with alcohol of varying severity.

Chapter 4: Mental health

Mental ill-health can be a major barrier to successful transition, and the current lack of effective care exacerbates already debilitating conditions.

⇨ Since 2007, up to 11,000 serving members of the military have been diagnosed with mental health conditions including post-traumatic stress disorder (PTSD) and depression;

⇨ In 2012, 2,550 soldiers, sailors, airmen and marines were treated for mental health issues whilst in uniform; of which 11 per cent were reports of PTSD but 21 per cent related to mood disorders such as depression;

⇨ In 2012, a total of 3,425 days were lost due to days spent in hospital;

⇨ 13,550 UK service personnel who had deployed to Iraq and/ or Afghanistan had at least one episode of care for a mental health disorder between 1 January 2007 and 30 June 2013.

Whilst PTSD is a major concern, the CSJ has heard that there is currently too heavy a focus on it, detracting from other significant problems, notably depression and stress. In 2005, 28.9 per cent of former service personnel self-reported as having had a mental health problem in service, of which depression (48.3 per cent) and stress (37.9 per cent) were the dominant conditions. A follow-up study in 2010 confirmed these trends, with alcohol misuse identified in 13 per cent of respondents, and common mental disorders in 19.7 per cent, far in excess of the PTSD rates of four per cent.

Certain groups within the military are far more vulnerable to suffering from mental ill health. 49.5 per cent of self-reporting service leavers with poor mental health held a junior rank when leaving, and 78.6 per cent had been in the Army. The potential warnings of the future impact of deploying reservists in large numbers, as recommended by the Forces 2020 review, are also clear. Current and former reservists are at greater risk of psychological illness than regulars as a result of their experiences. More than a quarter (26 per cent) of reservists deployed to Iraq had a mental disorder following deployment, and six per cent had PTSD as compared to 19 and four per cent respectively amongst regular counterparts.

Challenges still exist in the delivery of treatment to those who are currently still serving, in particular the issue of overcoming stigma that will allow those suffering to come forward and receive treatment. The consequences of not receiving treatment, and the interlinked nature of issues such as alcohol substance misuse, crime, family breakdown and homelessness, amongst others, can result in a destructive downward spiral that prevents re-integration into civilian life.

Chapter 5: Crime

Former members of the Armed Forces make up the largest single occupational group in UK prisons. In 2010, DASA estimated that 2,820, or 3.5 per cent, of the prison population had served in the Armed Forces. However, recent reports suggest that this may have risen to seven per cent. As of 13 December 2013, the UK's prison population was 85,255, meaning that approximately 5,970 once served in the Armed Forces, more than double DASA's estimate.

These numbers exist at considerable cost to the state. HMP Wandsworth, for example, reported a seven per cent respondent rate for those declaring themselves to be a former member of the Armed Forces. Their cost per prisoner based on direct expenditure alone would suggest that Wandsworth's ex-military population costs the taxpayer more than £2 million per year.

The overwhelming majority of these prisoners were from an Army background: in the DASA study, 77 per cent were ex-Army, 15 per cent served in the Royal Navy and Royal Marines, and eight per cent served with the RAF.

The types of crimes that are committed are also significant, with violence against the person being the most common conviction amongst former service personnel, with 33 per cent imprisoned for this offence.

Deployment to combat zones has certainly had an impact on the propensity for violent offending; those service personnel who have seen combat in Iraq and Afghanistan are more than twice as likely to commit a violent offence than those who have occupied non-frontline roles. Experience of a greater number of traumatic events also had a direct correlation to the committing of violent offences. In addition, experiences of combat and trauma during deployment were identified as being strongly associated with violent behaviour following homecoming after an operational deployment. Alcohol

plays a major role in these crimes, with 44 per cent of violent crimes in one study having been committed by those suffering from alcohol misuse.

As such, it is clear that the issue of former members of Armed Forces incarcerated in prisons is dominated by those who served amongst the lower ranks, a cohort that this report has already identified as being more vulnerable to struggling to re-integrate into civilian life.

Violence is inextricably linked to military service, and the preponderance of former soldiers in contact with the criminal justice system in the UK may well suggest an enduring pattern of behaviour that is in part established by service in the military.

For full references please see:

http://www.centreforsocialjustice.org.uk/UserStorage/pdf/Pdf%20reports/Military.pdf

April 2014

⇨ The above information has been reprinted with kind permission from The Centre for Social Justice. Please visit www.centreforsocialjustice.org.uk for further information.

© The Centre for Social Justice 2014

The lid has been lifted on poor veteran care – now we need to improve it

Article from The Conversation.

By Clarissa Giebel, Research Assistant and PhD Student in Cognitive Neuropsychology and Dementia at University of Manchester

THE CONVERSATION

Accusations are being made that the UK Government is failing to meet the very standards it set for itself when it comes to veterans. Medical experts say former military personnel are not being given the priority NHS treatment they were promised in the military covenant that was signed into law in 2011.

Orthopaedic surgeon Tim Biggs and psychiatry specialist Neil Greenberg have both been quoted as saying that promises being made about veteran care are not being realised. Former soldiers say they are facing difficulties in getting NHS treatment and shadow ministers say the government is failing in its duty.

But this problem is not just about missing out on treatment. When veterans do get help, it is often not the help they need. Services still target veterans as a group, rather than as individuals with very individual needs.

The trauma and stress that service in war zones can cause mean that what happens to personnel after they leave is actually one of the most important aspects of military service. They suddenly find themselves away from what has been a life of strict discipline and intense pressure and can struggle to cope with the transition. Services are available to help but they often fail to recognise that each veteran is different. Services need to be more tailored to reflect the different problems faced by former military personnel, be they old or young.

Services to support military veterans in this part of their lives were only introduced after World War I had ended. Back then, there was little help provided except what was offered by family and friends. But as governments started to experience the consequences of the psychological damage that can be done to personnel, they started paying large sums of money to develop proper services, such as the Ministry of Defence's Medical Assessment Programme. Services such as Combat Stress, The Veterans' Mental Health Charity, have also since been established.

Re-integration into society can be a tough social and psychological task. With or without the support of family and friends, veterans need to adjust to everyday life. They need to find housing and secure a stable income as well as access welfare services.

Differing needs

The general belief is that a veteran is someone who has served their whole career in the Army, the Royal Navy or the Royal Air Force before going into retirement. But in the UK, a veteran is someone who has served and received pay, even if it is just for one day. That means veterans can be in their very early 20s or well into their 90s.

Given this expansive age gap, and the overwhelming variety and magnitude of combat experiences veterans are likely to have faced during their time in active service, no two veterans are the same. Their experiences can shape their psychological profile and their needs differ on a case-by-case basis.

In a recent study, we evaluated the effect of a new clinical and social service for military veterans in the north-west of England. A few years ago, the Government introduced a scheme called Improving Access to Psychological Therapies, or IAPT. This was to support people in the general population who were suffering from depression and anxiety. The service we assessed in our study was the first to target IAPT therapy specifically at veterans.

We found that the success of a therapy was to some extent influenced by the type of veteran being treated. Those who had left the service early made more lasting recoveries from anxiety and depression, while those who had a physical disability or were abusing alcohol or drugs found it harder.

Although current services for veterans provide a variety of different treatments, such as self-help, cognitive behavioural therapy, stress exercises or medication, very little is known about how different types of veterans are treated. This is because ours is the first to have evaluated treatments for different subgroups within one study. We need to have a better understanding of those groups and their therapeutic outcomes before services can be adapted.

Anxiety and depression are a serious burden to society – and depression is a major cause of death in adults. We need to find ways to improve the benefits of therapy to reduce this toll. Veterans are exposed to different life situations that could trigger anxiety and depression – and that may be particularly true for the younger ones. If they leave the service early, they may have done so intentionally or for a specific reason so they may need more tailored care than someone who has simply spent their whole career in service and needs help adjusting.

Veterans might make up a small part of the population but they often experience mental health problems when trying to adjust to everyday life. To date, only a few veteran-specific services exist.

It's already clear that veterans need a different type of treatment to the general population because the problems they face are so closely linked to life in military service.

But it's also beginning to look like they need different treatments from each other. Some have served for decades while others have completed just one tour and come away traumatised. No two veterans are the same and we need to think in more detail about how to deal with their problems.

29 October 2014

⇨ The above information has been reprinted with kind permission from *The Conversation*. Please visit www.theconversation.com for further information.

Homeless veterans: 'wannabe warrior' claims stop real veterans getting help, warns charity boss

By Anna David, Education Editor

Veterans who fall on hard times could be prevented from getting help because of the number of people falsely claiming to have served in the armed forces, the head of a military charity has warned.

Dr Hugh Milroy, CEO of Veterans Aid, said he knew of cases where homeless people had pretended to be veterans or exaggerated their military service to win sympathy.

The phenomenon can stop real veterans from getting help because charities waste time on false claims, he said.

Dr Milroy, whose charity is one of those at the heart of the *Evening Standard*'s Homeless Veterans campaign, called for laws to be brought in making it harder for someone to pretend they served in the British military.

He said the Government should consider a UK equivalent to America's Stolen Valour Act, under which it is a crime to make false claims about military decorations.

He said: 'Medals are hard earned, and if someone is sporting a chest-full of medals that are made up, it demeans the whole process and breaks our trust with the public.'

In the UK, pretending to have served in the armed forces is only illegal if the person doing so stands to make a financial gain, for which they can be pursued for fraud.

The military charities supported by the Homeless Veterans campaign – Veterans Aid and ABF The Soldiers' Charity – can check if people are genuine by asking for a unique service number. But Dr Milroy warned smaller charities and the public can be fooled.

Professor Edgar Jones, a military psychiatrist at King's College London, said the idea of soldiers exaggerating the extent of their military service was a 'well-established phenomenon' but that recent wars in Iraq and Afghanistan had revived the problem.

He said: 'Popular culture is focused on "heroes" and "warriors". Service personnel have attracted a huge amount of public support. By putting on a uniform and pretending to be a veteran, it will attract sympathy.'

10 February 2015

⇨ The above information has been reprinted with kind permission from the *London Evening Standard*. Please visit www.standard.co.uk for further information.

Stolen Valor Act

In the United States it is a crime for a person to pretend they are a soldier when they are not, with the intention of claiming any kind of benefit (e.g. money, property, etc.). It is also a crime to make false claims about military decorations (e.g. medals). It is legal to wear a military uniform in public, as long as the person doesn't claim to have done any service.

The UK has a similar law.

What is the Armed Forces Covenant?

Issue

The Armed Forces Covenant sets out the relationship between the nation, the Government and the armed forces. It recognises that the whole nation has a moral obligation to members of the armed forces and their families, and it establishes how they should expect to be treated.

The covenant's two principles are that:

⇨ the armed forces community should not face disadvantage compared to other citizens in the provision of public and commercial services

⇨ special consideration is appropriate in some cases, especially for those who have given most, such as the injured and the bereaved.

The covenant exists to redress the disadvantages that the armed forces community may face in comparison to other citizens, and to recognise sacrifices made.

The Armed Forces Covenant is supported by the community covenant and the corporate covenant. The community covenant encourages local communities to support the armed forces community in their area and promote public understanding and awareness. The corporate covenant is a public pledge from businesses and other organisations who wish to demonstrate their support for the armed forces community.

Actions

The Ministry of Defence (MOD), together with other government departments, the devolved administrations, partner charities and voluntary organisations, has been working to fulfil the series of commitments we made to the armed forces community. The second annual report was published in December 2013 and sets out the progress we've made and the areas of disadvantage that still remain.

Actions taken so far

The actions we've taken so far include:

⇨ three tranches of the covenant LIBOR fund

⇨ making funding of £6.5 million available to guarantee that all serving personnel and veterans injured in Iraq or Afghanistan will be able to upgrade to the latest prosthetics technology, including the Genium bionic prosthetic system, where clinically appropriate

⇨ twice doubling council tax relief, it now stands at nearly £600 per service person for a six-month deployment

⇨ introducing a Service Pupil Premium, currently valued at £300 per child, for the children of service personnel

⇨ setting up an additional fund of £3 million per year, rising to £6 million per year from 2014 to 15, to support state schools catering for significant numbers of children of service personnel, including children of reservists

⇨ developing shadow postcodes for British Forces Post Office (BFPO) addresses so that service personnel can access online goods and services

⇨ launching the community covenant and the £30 million Community Covenant Grant Scheme for local projects

⇨ to date, spent £35 million from fines levied on banks for manipulating the LIBOR, for projects supporting the armed forces community

⇨ launching a new Defence Discount Service, which offers a privilege card entitling members of the armed forces community to a range of discounts on goods and services

⇨ launching the corporate covenant to foster stronger relationships between the armed forces community and businesses and charitable organisations.

Present and future actions

The Armed Forces Covenant is not an event but a process. The most recent annual report set out a number of areas where more work was required. Over the year ahead the Government will among other things:

⇨ introduce the new £200 million Forces Help to Buy Scheme

⇨ establish a fully operational Defence Primary Healthcare Service

⇨ extend access to the Standard Learning Credits Scheme to all members of the reserve forces from April 2014.

The importance of the covenant was demonstrated by the chancellor's decision to make funding for the covenant permanent. A further £10 million per year will be spent from 2015–16, on top of the £65 million already made available, with a further up to £100 million for the armed forces community and emergency services announced in the Chancellor's Autumn Statement.

Background

The Armed Forces Covenant recognises that the Government and the nation have an obligation to the armed forces community and it establishes how they should expect to be treated. It was published in May 2011 together with 'The Armed Forces Covenant: today and tomorrow' which detailed the steps being taken to support the armed forces community.

The Armed Forces Covenant itself is not a legal document but its key principles have been enshrined in law in the Armed Forces Act 2011. The legislation obliges the Defence Secretary to report annually on progress made by the Government in honouring the covenant.

We published the second annual report in December 2013. The report sets out the progress we've made and the areas of disadvantage that still remain.

Bills and legislation

The Armed Forces Act 2011 enshrined the principles of the covenant in law.

9 May 2015

⇨ The above information has been reprinted with kind permission from the Ministry of Defence. Please visit www.gov.uk for further information.

Armed Forces Covenant myth buster

It's NOT just a piece of paper

The Armed Forces Covenant was published in May last year along with a document called 'Today and Tomorrow' which lists the nearly 100 real, tangible commitments the Government has made to the Armed Forces Community.

It IS a Government priority

A Cabinet committee has had four meetings to check Ministers are delivering what they said they would, and the Prime Minister has been to two of these meetings.

It IS about fair treatment

The Covenant exists to make sure service people, veterans and their families are on an equal footing with ordinary citizens when it comes to accessing public and commercial services. For example, if you and your family are posted somewhere new, you shouldn't struggle to get your child into a local school. We've made sure that doesn't happen by letting schools go over their maximum class size to fit in a service child.

It's NOT about extra-special treatment for all the Forces

For most of the Armed Forces Community, the Covenant is about removing disadvantage so that you get the same outcome as the civilian community. It's not about getting special treatment that ordinary citizens wouldn't receive, or getting a better result.

It IS about special consideration in some cases

For those who have given the most, such as the injured and the bereaved, we do make an exception. For example we've made sure that service people with genital injuries are guaranteed three cycles of IVF on the NHS, and we've established a scholarship fund for bereaved service children.

It's NOT a legal document

The Armed Forces Covenant itself is not a legal document, but it is referenced in the Armed Forces Act 2011 and the Secretary of State for Defence is legally required to report to Parliament on its progress once a year.

It IS having an impact on the lives of the Armed Forces Community

A huge number of positive changes have been made since May 2011, but sometimes you might not recognise them as Covenant commitments. We've twice doubled council tax relief to nearly £600 for a six-month deployment, we've introduced BFPO postcodes to make it easier to access commercial products and we've given priority access to social housing for veterans, bereaved families and service people who need adapted homes.

It IS about local communities too

The Covenant is not just about the Government delivering commitments on a national level. More than 100 local communities have signed a Community Covenant. It is a voluntary statement of mutual support between civilians and the Armed Forces in their area to encourage mutual understanding and to bring the two communities together. Alongside it we run the Community Covenant Grant Scheme, set up to fund projects that support its aims.

It IS an obligation on the whole of society

The Covenant is an obligation on the whole of society. It includes voluntary and charitable bodies, private organisations and individuals, all of whom are asked to recognise our Armed Forces and offer respect, support and fair treatment.

⇨ The above information has been reprinted with kind permission from the Ministry of Defence. Please visit www.gov.uk for further information.

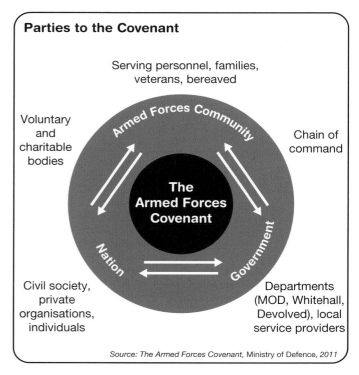

Parties to the Covenant

Serving personnel, families, veterans, bereaved

Voluntary and charitable bodies

Armed Forces Community

Chain of command

The Armed Forces Covenant

Nation

Government

Civil society, private organisations, individuals

Departments (MOD, Whitehall, Devolved), local service providers

Source: The Armed Forces Covenant, Ministry of Defence, 2011

The mental health of the UK Armed Forces

This briefing provides an outline of the current evidence on UK military mental health, including prevalence rates of mental health problems in serving personnel (regulars and reserves) and data on suicide, help-seeking, violence and offending.[1]

1. Impact of the operations in Iraq and Afghanistan

As yet, there is no evidence of a 'bow wave', 'tidal wave' or 'tsunami' of mental health problems in UK Regulars or Reservists. In 2004–6, there was no overall increase in mental health problems in Regular personnel who had served in Iraq compared to rest of the Armed Forces. Across the whole of the UK Armed Forces, the prevalence of probable post-traumatic stress disorder (PTSD) was around 4%. Despite increased deployments, prolonged operations in Iraq and increased commitment in Afghanistan, PTSD rates remained stable when assessed in 2007–9. Similar rates of probable PTSD were reported before, during and after deployment.

However, Regulars deployed in combat roles (in both 2004–6 and 2007–9) reported a higher prevalence of probable PTSD than those deployed in other roles (6.9% compared to 3.6%, in 2007–9).

In addition, Reservists reported higher rates of probable PTSD after deployment to Iraq compared to those not deployed (6% vs 3%, in 2004–6). The association with deployment remained in 2007–9 (5% in deployed vs. 2% in non-deployed). This is probably a result of different pre-deployment and homecoming experiences, rather than experiences in theatre. Reservists report feeling alienated from the military once they have been demobilised, which may be linked to continuing poor mental health. Recent evidence has shown that the increase in both probable PTSD and marital problems

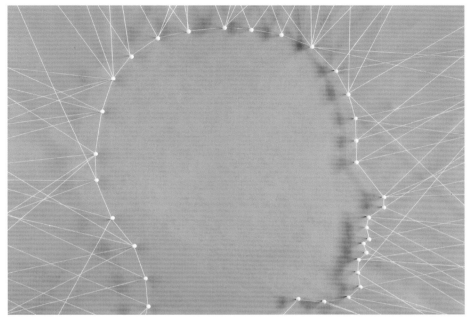

persists five years after deployment, which is cause for concern.

There is evidence of increased levels of alcohol misuse in Regulars post deployment both at phase 1 and phase 2 (16%) compared to the non-deployed (11%); especially those in combat roles (22%).

There has been an observed increase in absolute numbers of Service personnel and veterans visiting Defence Medical Services (DMS), Service charities and the NHS for help with mental health problems. There may be several reasons for this. First, it might simply be due to a true increase in rates of mental health problems. Second, it might reflect a modest success in reducing stigma associated with mental illness (as published data suggests this has reduced by about 5% since 2008). Third, it might be due to a decrease in time taken to seek help (as reported by charities). In addition, in-Service process changes have facilitated the referral process to DMS of patients with mental ill health.

US rates of PTSD and mild traumatic brain injury (mTBI) in Service personnel are higher than in the UK and are substantially increased

after deployment. This difference was probably due to higher combat exposure among US forces in earlier studies (a difference which disappeared as UK forces saw substantially more combat in Afghanistan), longer tour lengths, greater number of Reservists and age differences. Entitlement to post-Service healthcare provision may also play a role; with some exceptions, veterans require a Service-related diagnosis (and accompanying compensation) to access enhanced healthcare through Veterans Aid, which may encourage more to report ill-health.

In summary, there is no evidence of a tidal wave of deployment-related mental health problems.

2. Mental health overall

In general, there is no clear evidence that mental health in the Armed Forces is substantially worse than other occupational groups. However, whilst earlier research had suggested that there did not appear to be a difference in the rates of common mental health disorders between military personnel and civilians; more recent analysis has questioned that view. PTSD continues to be less common than either

1. The main data source for this briefing is the KCMHR cohort study. KCMHR completed two waves of questionnaire based data collection from UK Service personnel in 2004–6 (phase 1) and 2007–9 (phase 2), with the second phase also picking up recent Service leavers. These findings are supplemented with data from a range of other KCMHR research projects, research from Defence Statistics (Health) and US military health researchers, as well as open sources. The 300+ publications produced by KCMHR and ADMMH can be found at www.kcl.ac.uk/kcmhr/publications.

depression or anxiety (common mental health problems) or alcohol misuse; the latter continues to be the main problem for Armed Forces personnel.

Groups at increased risk of any mental health problem include Reservists, combat troops, those with pre-existing social or childhood adversities and early Service leavers (leaving before completing four years of service).

Members of the UK Armed Forces report considerably higher rates of alcohol misuse than the general population, especially within the Royal Navy and Army. The rates are also higher than those reported in the US or Australian militaries, which may be partly accounted for by demographics/ selection (e.g. differing recruitment patterns, and self-selection, whereby certain demographic groups may be more likely to sign up). Across all age groups, the relative frequency of hazardous drinking among military men is nearly twice that in the male general population and for women three times. These differences reduce with age. The pattern is of binge drinking and harmful use of alcohol (causing health, social and psychological harm). True alcohol dependence is unusual, perhaps because deployments are dry. Nevertheless, rates of dependence remain higher than the general population.

There is no evidence that the length of a single tour, or number of tours, has had an adverse effect on Service personnel's mental health, provided that Harmony Guidelines are followed. When the actual tour length exceeds the expected length, it has a substantial adverse impact on mental health and also alcohol misuse.

Whilst there is some evidence that severely physically injured Service personnel are at increased risk of mental health problems; the increased risk of these conditions is even more prominent in personnel who suffer from severe general medical conditions whilst deployed.

3. Suicide

Overall, rates of suicide are lower in the Armed Forces than they are in the general population. The only exception is an increased suicide rate in young men (under the age of 20) in the Army. Young veterans (aged 16–24)

or those classified as early service leavers are also at an increased risk of suicide. Evidence from several sources suggests that the increase in suicide risk in these two groups is mainly a result of pre-Service vulnerabilities, such as childhood adversity. The longer an individual stays in the military, the lower the suicide risk: long-serving personnel are an increasingly selected and resilient group.

Self-harm in Service personnel is mainly impulsive, is not associated with deployment and is a poor predictor of subsequent suicide risk.

It is not true that 'more Falklands Veterans died of suicide than in conflict'. Regardless of absolute numbers, what matters most is whether the suicide rate is higher among Falkland veterans compared to members of the Armed Forces who did not deploy to the Falklands, and higher than the general population. Defence Statistics (Health) has shown that this is not the case.

4. Screening

Pre-deployment mental health screening does not reduce the rate of post-deployment mental health problems.

A large, US-funded, randomised controlled trial of post-deployment mental health screening in Regular Service personnel is now in progress, and is being undertaken by KCMHR and ADMMH. Any decision about standardised post-deployment mental

health screening should await the results of this trial.

5. Help seeking

There are several definite barriers to help seeking for mental health problems among Service personnel, but stigma is particularly important; especially perceptions of how leaders and colleagues would view their seeking of help. Whilst education may help reduce public-stigma, reduction of self-stigma (the belief an individual holds about their own mental health) is more difficult and requires other approaches.

Officers report lower rates of help seeking than other ranks when they acknowledge a stress or emotional problem.

Barriers to care do not go away when Service personnel leave the Armed Forces. In fact, some get worse (e.g. seeking help for alcohol misuse). Mental health stigma is a general problem across society, and is not specific to the UK Armed Forces. The same has been found in the US and Canadian militaries and the Australian Defence Force. There is evidence that whole-force stigma reporting has modestly declined since 2008. Stigmatising beliefs are, however, more commonly reported by personnel during operations than when they are back home.

Only a minority of veterans with mental health problems receive NICE-

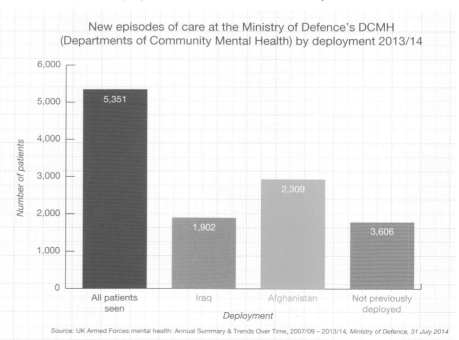

New episodes of care at the Ministry of Defence's DCMH (Departments of Community Mental Health) by deployment 2013/14

Source: UK Armed Forces mental health: Annual Summary & Trends Over Time, 2007/09 – 2013/14, Ministry of Defence, 31 July 2014

approved treatments. Recent evidence suggests that many GPs are aware of the Service background of most recent Service leavers, but lack treatment and referral options. The pattern of mental health problems (non-psychosis, comorbid with high rates of substance misuse, crossing the boundaries into problems with employment, debt, housing, offending, etc.) are areas less well served by either NHS primary care or specialist mental health services.

6. Violence and offending

Defence Statistics (Health) estimates that 3.5% of the current prison population have served in the UK military. This is slightly lower than expected. However, ex-Servicemen still constitute a significant subset of the adult male prison population and are the largest occupational group. They are also more likely to be in prison for a sex offence or violence against the person than the general population. Rates of acquisitive offending are, however, lower than the general population.

Self-reported violence is increased in the post-deployment period and is associated with pre-Service adversity, as well as alcohol and PTSD. Those who have served in a combat role are twice as likely to report violence on return from deployment than those who were not exposed to combat. However, higher levels of pre-enlistment adversity and deployment-related mental health problems may account for much of this increased risk.

The picture is similar for actual convictions recorded on the Police National Computer. Those who have served have a lower lifetime rate of criminal convictions than those who have not. This is remarkable when one considers the social backgrounds of many who serve. However, this is not true for violent convictions, which are increased. The main associations are predictable – age, gender, previous convictions, etc. Violent offending is not associated with deployment per se, but is associated with combat, even taking into account the fact that having a combat role is not random (recruitment for combat roles tends to be clustered around areas with higher levels of social deprivation), and more people with prior problems go into combat arms. This link is mediated by

alcohol, traumatic exposures and, to a lesser extent, PTSD.

7. Relevant in-Service policy initiatives

The Veterans and Reservists' Mental Health Programme at Chilwell was set up in response to KCMHR findings on Reservists' mental health. Uptake is low, but the service appears to be clinically and occupationally effective.

Stigma and reluctance to access services is being addressed by peer group support (trauma risk management, or 'TRiM'). A randomised controlled trial on this programme found that the programme did not cause harm but did not alter reported stigma over an 18-month period. TRiM is, however, a safe and acceptable approach, and is now being used in other organisations. TRiM appears to help people to access social support and in non-military studies its use is associated with a reduction in traumatic-event related sickness absence.

In theatre, good leadership, morale and cohesion are the main determinants of good mental health. Events at home (e.g. relationship issues) are as important as combat exposure. The deployment of mental health professionals is associated with good occupational outcomes. These results have been used by the Permanent Joint Headquarters to support in-theatre mental health provision.

Approaches to improving post-deployment adjustment have included third location decompression (a stop-off in Cyprus on the way back to the UK) and 'Battlemind' (a post-deployment mental health intervention). Decompression is popular (after the event) and there is some evidence to suggest that it reduces mental health problems. In a trial, Battlemind did not reduce rates of PTSD, but it did have a modest effect on alcohol use.

8. Conclusions

⇨ Overall, the mental health of UK Armed Forces personnel remained stable between 2004–6 and 2007–9, despite increases in Operational Tempo and the number of deployments.

⇨ But deployed Reservists and deployed Regulars who have seen

combat report higher rates of probable PTSD after deployment.

⇨ Regulars show an increased risk of alcohol misuse after deployment.

⇨ There is no tidal wave/bow wave of mental health problems in the UK military as yet, but the workload of DMS, charities and the NHS will increase.

⇨ Stigma remains a barrier to help-seeking for serving and ex-Service personnel. There is no evidence that stigma is worse because of a Service background. Stigma is not a static concept – it changes; for example, before, during and after deployment.

⇨ Evidence is emerging that Service personnel and veterans are now seeking help earlier from both DMS and Service charities. This may reflect changes in society and also an impact of anti-stigma campaigns. Increased numbers seeking help against a stable overall level of mental health problems, determined by true population studies, may be a sign of success, not failure, provided that no overall population increases are found in the future.

⇨ Most Service leavers do well. Those who do not have multiple overlapping health and social problems (debt, unstable housing, unemployment, violence, substance misuse, deliberate self-harm). Most poor outcomes are compressed into the Early Service Leavers (who served for less than four years). Present policy gives the most resettlement support to those who have served the longest, rather than those most in need.

October 2014

⇨ The above information has been reprinted with kind permission from King's Centre for Military Health Research and Academic Department for Military Mental Health (KCMHR and ADMMH). Please visit www.kcl.ac.uk/kcmhr for further information.

Veterans bring 'military ethos' to schools

Growing number of organisations employ ex-servicemen and women to work in schools helping children develop 'character'.

By Sally Weale, education correspondent

The pupils of year five at St Aloysius Catholic primary in Roby, Liverpool stand shoulder to shoulder, listening closely as the man in combat trousers and army boots outlines the task ahead.

Dressed in their blue PE shorts and white tops, they stand tall as the instructor speaks. First they have to imagine they are stranded in a desert and work out what they need to survive.

The man in charge of operations, Wayne Barker, used to be a corporal in the Royal Signals, serving ten years as a communications expert and physical training instructor, putting regiments of 450 soldiers through their paces. He has done tours of Afghanistan and Iraq, and used to live in Germany.

Now, for more than a year, he has been spending three days a week at St Aloysius, bringing the 'military ethos' to the school hall and classrooms, instilling 'character' in little girls with intricate plaits, and boys with eczema scabs behind their knees.

Barker, 29, is employed by Commando Joe's, one of a small but growing number of organisations that employ mainly ex-servicemen and women to work in schools with the aim of helping children develop 'character' and 'resilience'.

'Dressed in their blue PE shorts and white tops, they stand tall as the instructor speaks. First they have to imagine they are stranded in a desert and work out what they need to survive'

These are the new buzzwords at the Department for Education (DfE). Among politicians and policymakers there seems to be a sense that children are lacking the 'grit' required in the modern world.

In December the Education Secretary, Nicky Morgan, announced £4.8 million of funding for projects such as Commando Joe's to help schools instil character in pupils. This month the department invited schools to put themselves forward for the 2015 DfE character awards, with a £20,000 prize.

So how does it work in practice? Barker is known to the children not as Wayne, or Mr Barker, but as Commando Joe. His day starts with a breakfast club; then he visits every class to chase up attendance and punctuality, during school assembly he does a five-to-ten-minute 'wake and shake' session for the whole school (including staff), then he works in class directed by a teacher, mentoring small groups.

At break time he's in the playground 'providing a positive male role model presence', then he's in the imaginary desert with year five, focusing on 'team building, resilience, bounce back and acceptance of rules and communication'.

At lunchtime he helps staff supervise the queue, then, according to the schedule, 'Commando Joe invites specially chosen pupils to have dinner with him as a reward and allows them to attend Commando Joe's VIP table where we discuss manners, behaviour and the school day'. In reality it's more relaxed.

When *The Guardian* visits, Barker splits the children into teams – one will build a shelter, the other an aqueduct to transport water from an oasis to the shelter. 'Anybody know what an oasis is?' he asks.

'Is it a drink?' asks one boy.

'The band?' suggests another.

Barker explains which oasis he is referring to then the timed mission begins and the children spring into action. By the end of the session, they manage (with help) to build a creditable shelter that all of them can fit in without collapse, and a slightly wonky aqueduct.

The Shadow Education Secretary, Tristram Hunt, has also stressed the importance of character, recently telling a conference on the subject: 'The great British spirit comes from our ability to overcome adversity and setbacks,' he said. 'Character, resilience and the ability to bounce back: it's what makes us British.'

Mike Hamilton started Commando Joe's in 2009 after eight years in the Royal Engineers, working in bomb disposal, in Iraq, Afghanistan and Northern Ireland. He did a spell working with an outreach team going into secondary schools to promote the military, but felt 'conflicted' about being involved in recruitment.

So he dreamt up Commando Joe's, went on the BBC TV show *Dragons' Den* and asked for £50,000 funding from James Caan and Duncan Bannatyne. They turned him down so Hamilton went his own way and it was the DfE that eventually came up with the money – £600,000 in 2011–12, £1 million the following year and another million in the latest round of funding. Now he has 62 mainly male instructors of whom all but 11 are ex-military, working in 256 primary and secondary schools. With the latest funding Hamilton is hoping to expand to 375 schools around the country, employing a further 20-plus instructors.

Even he's slightly uneasy about the military element and experimented with substituting camouflage trousers with dark trousers. 'But the parents thought we were the police and wouldn't talk to us,' says Hamilton. Instructors do occasionally get asked by older children about their army careers and how many people they've killed, but in primaries it rarely comes up.

Not everyone is relentlessly enthusiastic about introducing a military ethos into the schools. Christine Blower, General Secretary of the National Union of Teachers agrees developing character and resilience is an important aspect of the work in schools, but says: 'A military ethos is certainly not the only way to achieve this.'

Organisations such as ForcesWatch, which scrutinises the ethics of military recruitment, have expressed their concern and the Quakers have written to Morgan condemning what they describe as the 'ongoing militarisation of education'.

'Quakers believe that military ethos is not what young people need,' says the letter. 'While it claims to engender altruism, aspiration and teamwork, these are not the exclusive preserve of the military. A military culture is one of blind obedience, not the critical thinking learners need, and is founded on the normalisation of violence.'

The headteacher at St Aloysius, Sheryl Wrigley, says she doesn't really notice the military aspect of Commando Joe's and is so pleased with Barker's work that she has tripled his days. 'We started with one day per week, then two, then three,' says Wrigley. 'We don't have any male teaching staff which is a big issue for us.

'I'm from a sporting background and I like that whole approach of team building and being there for each other, that resilience, learning how to face defeat and carry on. That was really important for us – giving the children skills for the future to help them to cope.'

How does she measure the scheme's success? 'We had a number of year six boys last year who were very difficult to engage in their learning. Then Wayne developed a sports leadership programme for them.' They were given the responsibility to organise lunchtime coaching sessions for the younger children, including a tournament with awards, and it transformed their attitude to school. While the Government has boosted organisations like Commando Joe's, the school still has to pay for it to provide staff. It costs £200 a day to employ him – more than £23,000 a year, paid for out of the pupil premium funding St Aloysius receives for disadvantaged children.

'For what you get back, it's money well spent,' says Wrigley. 'We all love him.'

22 January 2015

⇨ The above information has been reprinted with kind permission from *The Guardian*. Please visit www.theguardian.com for further information.

> ## What is 'military ethos'?
> Military ethos can be thought of as the 'spirit' of the military; this refers to characteristics such as building character, resilience, self-discipline and teamwork.

Why are ex-servicemen over represented in prison?

This week's guest blog is written by Kevin Straughan, Deputy Director for Offender Learning (East Midland Region), Milton Keynes College.

Working with prisoners through our Offender Learning and Skills Service (OLASS), it has become clear to me that ex-servicemen are over represented in the criminal justice system.

Why do these intelligent, often well educated, and indeed capable men and women fall into offending behaviour upon leaving the services?

As an ex-serviceman myself, I know only too well the high intensity training recruits undertake. The army is about engaging in warfare, and the training involves the development of controlled aggression, and full conditioning for the role. Many have spent a lifetime in the services and leave still programmed to be a risk taker, sometimes aggressive, and often find themselves isolated from community and society in general.

A few begin to engage in crime, connected to the thrill seeking that goes with it. An example of this is an ex-Special Forces soldier who left the forces and began robbing banks, not purely for financial gain, but for the excitement he felt was missing from his life post-army.

Many ex-service personnel struggle to find work. Although they may have the skills required for a job, they don't have the relevant experience. Some that do find work, often their first civilian job, can't hold the job down and being resourceful and capable individuals, turn to offending behaviour to make money.

The breakdown of marriages, often resulting in homelessness, can also prove a catalyst for crime. The institutionalised background does little to help those who leave the forces, and although ex-service personnel are not necessarily more disadvantaged than anyone else, they do seem to end up in trouble more often.

So what can be done to help? More needs to be done to prepare people for release from the armed forces. It's getting better – as a society we have got better at recognising the issues and problems they face, but not better at providing the detailed support they require. Mental health charities are abundant, but the stigma attached to admitting such a problem is too great for many ex-service personnel to seek help. Individual armed services must take much more responsibility for resettlement and the military de-programming and normalisation which needs to take place.

Prisons have a responsibility to work with ex-forces staff in a different way. The nation has a charter with ex-services to provide advice, help and access to opportunities when needed. However, when individuals go to prison the charter seems to end. I'd like to see a charter for ex-service prisoners to enable them to get the same opportunity to develop and move forward as their non-offending peers.

My own personal experience of military life was that I was trained to do a specific job for many years; to be aggressive, to believe I was the best and that I was invincible. I left the institution to join the big wide world where I realised I was one of 80 million people, and all of that meant nothing. As a reasonably intelligent and resourceful individual, it really hit me. I had lost all my status – I was something in the army but when I left I felt that I had become absolutely nothing, just ordinary like everyone else and it took me a long time to realise ordinary is normal. I look at my peers who leave and are not able to cope and realise that the forces must get much better at recognising the signs of being unable to cope with the transition, and to do something about it on an individual basis.

So from an Offender Learning viewpoint, what can we do to help? My own transition is an example of coping with the cultural change that ex-service personnel have to face. Mine started when I realised who I really was; having to take an awful job when I left the army to discover my own strengths and weaknesses and to identify clearly a career route that provided self-actualisation and success. We need to provide that kind of journey for all ex-service personnel, and particularly for those in prison, which provides them with an opportunity to start again effectively and explore what they want to do with their lives. Some already have excellent academic and vocational qualifications, and we need to capitalise on that and work with them to engage in the labour market and to channel all of those transferable skills into a job.

12 December 2014

⇨ The above information has been reprinted with kind permission from NoOffence! Please visit www.no-offence.org for further information.

UK veterans and the criminal justice system

Executive summary

In comparison to the United States (US) there has been a lack of reliable research on the subject of the United Kingdom's (UK) veterans and the criminal justice system. However, Defence Analytical Services and Advice (DASA) have recently provided some useful evidence and there is a promising study, from Kings Centre for Military Health Research (KCMHR), in the pipeline. Despite this, our understanding of this subject matter is quite poor and there is a need to explore veterans' pathways to offending. This might be best achieved through a qualitative study of the experiences of veterans in UK prisons.

There is some debate about the presence of veterans in the prisons of England and Wales but the most reliable evidence suggests there are 2,820 individuals making up 3.5% of the total prison population.

Using these figures, veterans are 30% less likely to be in prison in England and Wales than non-veterans. Comparatively, veterans in the US are also less likely to be in prison than non-veterans.

Veterans in English and Welsh prisons are sentenced for a wide range of offences but the most common are violence against the person, sexual offences and drugs. This is broadly similar to the situation in the US. UK veterans are less likely to be in prison than non-veterans for all offence types except for sexual offences.

There is little evidence to support the common assumption that experience of conflict increases the likelihood of violent behaviour post-Service, although there is some proof that it leads to increased levels of risk-taking behaviour.

⇨ The above information has been reprinted with kind permission from The Royal British Legion. Please visit www.britishlegion.org.uk for further information.

© The Royal British Legion 2015

UK veterans and homelessness

Executive summary

There is quite a significant body of research on the subject of homelessness as experienced by veterans of the UK Armed Forces. This provides for a good understanding of both the size of the problem and the experiences of those involved.

The proportion of veterans among London's single homeless population is estimated to have fallen from above 20% in the mid to late 1990s, down to 6% in 2008. In terms of the number of veterans, this is a reduction from an estimate of between 3,000 and 4,000 down to approximately 1,100. This has been attributed to a combination of reduced output from the Armed Forces, improved Ministry of Defence (MoD) resettlement provision and better intervention from ex-Service charities.

The characteristics, profile and experiences of homeless veterans are largely the same as those of the wider homelessness population, although there are some notable differences. Homeless veterans have been found on average to be older, have slept rough for longer, be less likely to use drugs and more likely to have alcohol-related problems. Post-Traumatic Stress Disorder (PTSD) has been found among a small number of homeless veterans although other non-military related mental health problems were more common.

There is little evidence to support the notion that military life, or institutionalisation, is a cause of veterans' homelessness. There is some evidence that, for a minority, military life, through factors such as trauma of combat, mobility of the job or the drinking culture, had reduced their ability to cope post-Service.

In some cases, military life had suspended the impact of pre-existing vulnerabilities and these had resurfaced post-discharge. However, in the main, homelessness had occurred some time after Service. In common with the wider homeless population, a variety of factors and events had influenced and preceded homelessness.

⇨ The above information has been reprinted with kind permission from The Royal British Legion. Please visit www.britishlegion.org.uk for further information.

© The Royal British Legion 2015

Key facts

- The Naval Service has five components: Surface Ships; the Submarine Service; the Fleet Air Arm; the Royal Marines; and the Royal Fleet Auxiliary. (page 1)

- 45% of the Naval Service is actively deployed globally at any time. (page 1)

- The British Army consists of Regular Forces and Volunteer Reserves. There are currently over 89,000 Full-time Serving Personnel and over 24,000 Volunteer Reserves. (page 2)

- In 2015, the RAF will consist of around 33,000 full-time regular RAF personnel and 1,800 part-time reserve personnel. (page 2)

- Two thirds of the British public think that Post Traumatic Stress Disorder (PTSD) is much more common among the armed forces than among the general public. Actually, studies show that levels are similar – yet only 6% guess this fact correctly. (page 4)

- 72% have a favourable view of soldiers and 65% have a favourable view of the armed forces. (page 4)

- On an international level, attitudes towards the armed forces in the US are more positive (where 80% say they are favourable). British views are similar to Canada and Australia, but significantly more positive than in France (where only 52% say they have a favourable view of soldiers). (page 4)

- The risk of psychological harm in the army is higher than the risk of physical injury or death. (page 6)

- By 2020 the UK military will have a full time requirement of 142,500 personnel (British Army 82,000, Royal Navy 29,000 and Royal Air Force 31,500). (page 8)

- Every job/role in the UK military has a minimum and maximum age limit. The minimum age can differ between jobs/roles and is specified within each job description. However, the earliest application is at least 15 years and 9 months old when an individual applies, being at least 16 years old on entry and under 37 years old when beginning basic training (although the maximum age is typically around 30 years of age). (page 9)

- More than one in ten new Army recruits are boy soldiers of just 16 years old, according to the latest figures released by the Ministry of Defence (25 May 2014). (page 15)

- The Ministry of Defence is implementing £10.6 billion budget cuts which will lead to regular soldiers being slimmed down from 102,000 to 82,000 by 2020. (page 17)

- Between April 2013 to April 2014, the number of trained reservists increased by just 170 people. (page 17)

- The UK currently spends £37.4 billion on defence. However, 53% of those surveyed by PricewaterhouseCoopers (PwC) indicated they would like that to rise. This compares with 16% who would like to see the budget cut, while 21% said they think it should remain the same. (page 19)

- An Israeli study, based on numerous sources of information available between 2002 and 2005, examined the integration of female combatants in the IDF. It reported that Commanders recognise that female combatants often exhibit superior skills in areas including discipline and motivation, maintaining alertness, shooting abilities, managing tasks in an organised manner, and displaying knowledge and professionalism in the use of weapons. (page 21)

- Before 2000, openly gay people were banned from service, and those who suspected personnel of being gay had a duty to report them to authorities. (page 23)

- About 10% of the army is made up of black, Asian and ethnic minority people but many have joined from Commonwealth countries rather than the UK. (page 24)

- Estimates suggest that as many as six per cent of the current UK homeless population could be ex-Armed Forces. (page 25)

- Research published in 2007 found levels of alcohol consumption that are hazardous to physical and mental health amongst 67 per cent of men and 49 per cent of women in the British Armed Forces, far higher rates than those found in their civilian counterparts of 38 and 16 per cent for men and women, respectively. (page 27)

- In 2012, 2,550 soldiers, sailors, airmen and marines were treated for mental health issues whilst in uniform; of which 11 per cent were reports of PTSD but 21 per cent related to mood disorders such as depression. (page 27)

- Former members of the Armed Forces make up the largest single occupational group in UK prisons... As of 13 December 2013, the UK's prison population was 85,255, meaning that approximately 5,970 once served in the Armed Forces. (page 29)

Armed Forces

The Armed Forces consists of the Army (the British Army consists of Regular Forces and Volunteer Reserves), naval service (The Royal Navy and the Royal Marines) and the Royal Air Force. The purpose of these military forces is to strengthen international peace and security.

Armed Forces Covenant

The Armed Forces Covenant sets out the relationship between the nation, the Government and the armed forces. The covenant exists to redress the disadvantages that the armed forces community may face in comparison to other citizens, and to recognise sacrifices made. The covenant's two principles are that: the armed forces community should not face disadvantage compared to other citizens in the provision of public and commercial services; and special consideration is appropriate in some cases, especially for those who have given most, such as the injured and the bereaved.

Civilian

Anyone who is not a member of the military.

Civvy street

An informal phrase sometimes used by servicepeople and veterans to describe life and work outside of the military ('civvy' being short for 'civilian').

Close combat

In a battle situation, this refers to fighting between two combatants at short range.

Deployment

The movement of military personnel into an area of operation (such as a combat zone).

Discharge (from the armed forces)

A discharge is given to a member of the Armed Forces when their obligation to serve is over, releasing them from duty. There are different types of discharge, including Honourable and Dishonourable.

Military ethos

This spirit of the military; this refers to characteristics such as building character, resilience, self-discipline and teamwork.

Operations

Military actions in response to a developing situation or crisis.

Post-Traumatic Stress Disorder (PTSD)

PTSD is a psychological reaction to a highly traumatic event. It has been known by different names at different times in history: during the First World War, for example, soldiers suffering from PTSD were said to have 'shell shock'.

Regulars

Soldiers and officers of the regular Army ('regulars') are full-time military personnel. The regulars are distinct from those who serve in the Territorial Army, who train in their spare time.

Stolen Valor Act

In the United States it is a crime for a person to claim and pretend they are a soldier when they are not, with the intention of claiming any kind of benefit (e.g. money, property, etc.). It is legal to wear a military uniform in public, as long as the person doesn't claim to have done any service. There is a similar law in the UK.

Strategic Defence and Security Review

The SDSR was published by the Coalition Government in October 2010. It has caused much controversy, outlining large-scale budget cuts and redundancies within the Armed Forces. However, the Government says these are necessary for the Ministry of Defence to eliminate its estimated £38 billion deficit.

Territorial Army

Territorial soldiers and officers train in their spare time to provide support to full-time regular units when they're needed. There are two types of Territorial Unit – Regional and National. Regional Units train on week nights and some weekends and recruit from the local area. National Units tend to be more specialised and recruit people with relevant experience from all over the country. Because members travel further to get to training, they don't train on week nights. Most Army jobs are open to Territorials.

Veteran

A former serving member of the Armed Forces, in particular one who has given service during conflict or in time of war (more widely, the term 'veteran' is sometimes applied to anyone who has had long service in a particular field – people often talk about 'a veteran actor', for example).

Assignments

Brainstorming

⇨ In small groups, discuss what you know about the Armed Forces. Consider the following points:

- What services does the Armed Forces in the UK consist of?

- What do the Armed Forces do?

- What is the Territorial Army?

- What does 'military ethos' mean to you?

- What is the Stolen Valor Act?

Research

⇨ Find out about the condition of PTSD throughout history, beginning in the First World War. How was 'shell shock' diagnosed and treated? How has the way this illness is perceived changed since the early years of the 20th century? Do you think there is still a degree of stigma attached to this problem? Write a summary of your research findings.

⇨ Find out about the operations in Iraq and Afghanistan. What gave rise to the conflicts in these regions, and what part do British service personnel have to play? How many UK troops are currently stationed in these areas? Write a summary of British involvement in each conflict.

⇨ Find out about the work of the Territorial Army and write a summary of how they operate and in what way they complement the regular Army.

⇨ Choose a fact from this book which interests you the most and create a graph that illustrates its information.

Design

⇨ Design a poster that will raise awareness of the role of the Armed Forces both nationally and internationally.

⇨ Using articles concerning life after service, and the website www.civvystreet.org, create an illustrated booklet aimed at those about to leave the Armed Forces, entitled 'Life on Civvy Street'. Make sure you include information on where former service people can look for help and support.

⇨ Choose one of the articles in this book and create an illustration to highlight the key themes/message of your chosen article.

⇨ Design a website that will give parents information about programmes which use the 'military ethos' to help disadvantaged children (e.g. like how joining the cadets could be beneficial or how organisations like SkillForce work). Think about the kind of information they might need and give your site a name and logo.

Oral

⇨ 'This house believes it is not appropriate for young people under the age of 18, who are not able to join the police or watch an 18-rated war film, to nevertheless be allowed to join the Armed Forces.' Debate this motion in two groups, with one group arguing in favour and the other against.

⇨ 'We demand greater spending on the military.' Debate this motion as a class, with one group arguing in favour and the other against.

⇨ The mental health of the Armed Forces is a big issue. Do some research on the matter and create a five-minute presentation that explores your findings and share them with your class. You could include images, videos, maps and statistics to engage your audience.

⇨ As a class, discuss the role of women in the Armed Forces. Why is there so much controversy surrounding this issue? Should/can woman be in combat roles? Why or why not?

⇨ On an international level, attitudes towards the armed forces in the US are more positive (where 80% say they are favourable) than in the UK – some organisations even offer discounts to servicepersons. Why do you think this is? What is the public perception of armed forces in the UK? Do you think servicepeople deserve more respect and recognition, or are they 'just doing their job'? Discuss as a class.

Reading/writing

⇨ Write a one-paragraph definition of the Armed Forces.

⇨ Read *Mrs Dalloway* by Virginia Woolf, focusing in particular on the character of Septimus, the war veteran struggling to cope with PTSD, and the way in which his condition is treated by the medical establishment of the day. Write a review of the book and its portrayal of PTSD.

⇨ Read the articles concerning the Armed Forces Covenant. Do you think it is right for members and former members of the Armed Forces to be given special treatment in certain situations? Write an essay discussing your views.

⇨ Watch the final episode of the BBC TV series *Blackadder Goes Forth*. How does this manage to combine humour and poignancy in its portrayal of war?

⇨ Imagine you work for a charity which helps veterans integrate back into society (back to 'civvy street'). Write a blog-post for your charity's website explaining the issues surrounding veteran care and your feelings about the issue.

⇨ Write a diary entry from the perspective of a military veteran. What do you think your future will be like? How do you feel? How do you feel about society?

Acknowledgements

The publisher is grateful for permission to reproduce the material in this book. While every care has been taken to trace and acknowledge copyright, the publisher tenders its apology for any accidental infringement or where copyright has proved untraceable. The publisher would be pleased to come to a suitable arrangement in any such case with the rightful owner.

Images

All images courtesy of iStock, except page 2: MorgueFile, page 9 © UK Ministry of Defence and page 12 © JD Mac.

Illustrations

Don Hatcher: pages 7 & 37. Simon Kneebone: pages 17 & 25. Angelo Madrid: pages 1 & 10.

Additional acknowledgements

Editorial on behalf of Independence Educational Publishers by Cara Acred.

With thanks to the Independence team: Mary Chapman, Sandra Dennis, Christina Hughes, Jackie Staines and Jan Sunderland.

Cara Acred

Cambridge

September 2015